Your Free

We want to thank you for purchasing the book and would like to reward you with a valuable free gift

Food Styling Tips and Tricks

Just visit http://nb3publish.weebly.com to download it now.

We hope you enjoy it!

Thanks!

Archie Owens

Table of Contents

Easy Appetizer/Snack Ideas 9
   1. Fried Chicken 9
   2. Delicious Chicken Fried in Egg and Flour 11
   3. Dijon Lime Chicken 13
   4. Chicken Wings 15
   5. Fried Breakfast Sausage 17
   6. Simple Sausage Patties 19
   7. Meatballs with Yogurt 21
   8. Banana Peppers with Salami Roll Ups 23
   9. Mozzarella Sticks 25
   10. Fish Sticks 27
   11. Cinnamon Apple Chips 29
   12. Sweet Potato Slices 31
   13. Parmesan Crumbed Fish 33
   14. Salmon Burgers 35
   15. Coconut Shrimp Skewers 37
Vegetarian Appetizer/Snack 39
   16. Kale Chips 39
   17. Swedish Bean Curd Meatballs 41
   18. Veggie Vegetable Fries 43
   19. Honey Brussells Sprouts with Pecans 45
   20. Gujiya 47
Lunch/Dinner Ideas 49
   21. Chicken and Zucchini Ranch Meatballs with Potatoes 49
   22. Turkey Meatballs with Tomato Gravy 52
   23. Spicy Party Meatballs in Tomato Sauce 55
   24. Chicken Lasagna 58
   25. Balsamic Chicken with Veggies 61
   26. Honey Chicken Wings 64
   27. Garlic Parsley Potatoes 66
   28. Potato Creamy Casserole Gratin 68
   29. Stuffed Sweet Potatoes 70
   30. Avocado Fries 72
   31. Reuben Casserole 74
   32. Easy Steak with Mushrooms 76

33. Chipotle Beef..78
34. Steak and Pepper Sauce with Fried Chips..............................80
35. Glazed Salmon...82
36. Miso Tilapia..84
Vegetarian Lunch/Dinner...86
37. Herby Veggie Falafel with Pumpkin Sauce 86
38. Falafel with Tahini Sauce..89
39. Broccoli with Parmesan Cheese 92
40. Easy Vegetarian Lasagna 94
41. Zucchini and Halloumi Fritters..97
42. Macaroni and Cheese Toasties..99
43. Honey Cauliflower..101
44. Healthy Mediterranean Vegetables....................................104
45. Easy Crispy Tofu...106
Quick and Easy Dessert Recipes...108
46. Banana Spring Rolls...108
47. Brown Sugar Peaches...110
48. Chocolate Cake..112
49. Vegan Apple Turnover...114
50. Vegan Anzac Cookies..118
Conclusions..120

Introduction

Thank you for purchasing an Air Fryer Cookbook. You can now cook healthy, nutritious and tasty meals using carefully selected 50 recipes.

Most of us like nice crispy texture, but are shy on fried food using much oil to cook the food. Thus, when cooking French fries, one has to use quite a lot of oil, and even taking healthy fats, you still need to use plenty of oil to ensure that the fries are submerged into it. So, if you still want to enjoy crispy dishes but dislike much oil, the answer is in your Air Fryer!

You can now cook your French fries, chicken, fish, meat among many other dishes without using as much oil. Pour just a few tablespoons of oil and proceed!
Enjoy your time with your Air Fryer and our book of recipes!

What are Air Fryer and Air Frying

If it is new to you, here's what an air fryer looks like:

It is a countertop convection oven. This kitchen appliance employs superheated air to cook foods, yielding food, which is very similar to that obtained by high-temperature roasting. In a standard oven, the hot air cooks the food. Instead, in a convection air fryer, the heated air is blown around by a fan. This allows for cooking faster and more evenly when the food browns better and crisps up on the outside. Air fryers use the technology, which is essentially similar to that used in convection ovens. However, instead of blowing the air around a large rectangular box in standard ovens, it is circulated around in a compact cylinder, which is a more natural shape for the air circulation. The food sits in a perforated basket placed inside the cylinder. This appears to be much more efficient for cooking, creating an intense environment of heat and results in a food with a crispy brown exterior and moist tender interior. The result is similar to deep-frying, but without oil and fat needed to deep-fry.

Moreover, an air fryer doesn't just cook foods that are usually deep-fried. It can cook any foods that you would normally cook in your standard or microwave oven as well. It's great for so many different foods!

Furthermore, air frying is a great tool for reheating foods without making them rubbery, also being a convenient means to prepare ingredients.

To maximize the Air Fryer's cooking surface and include skewers to make vegetable or meat kabobs, you can use Airfryer Double Layer Rack. Non-Stick Baking Dish and Fry/Grill Pan are also very convenient supplements.

Health Benefits

The health benefits are apparent, based on a tiny amount of oil used. Deep frying involves submerging a food in hot oil, which is inevitably absorbed by the food. In an air fryer, one still uses oil, which helps fry up the food crisp and brown, but just one tablespoon is really needed at a time. You can simply toss dishes with the tablespoon of oil, and then place them in the air fryer basket. Another great idea is spraying the foods lightly with oil utilizing a kitchen spray bottle, which is the easiest way to get foods evenly coated with a small amount of oil.

Quick and Energy Efficient, Safe and Easy to Use

It is well known that one has to pre heat the standard oven to the temperature setting that is recommended before placing the food, which usually takes about 15 to 20 minutes. As the air fryer is compact, the preheat time is much less, from about 2 to 3 minutes. This makes seriously big energy savings.

Air frying is not only faster but also safer and easier than deep frying. One would simply set values of both time and temperature and then press the Start button. Doesn't get much easier than this! When deep frying, one has to heat a considerable amount of oil, which is dangerous, hard, and cumbersome to drain out.

Using the Digital Panel

Control panel example for HF-509TS, HF-959TS & HF-196TS AirFryer XL models is given below. It consists of a LED display, mode indicators, and function keys:

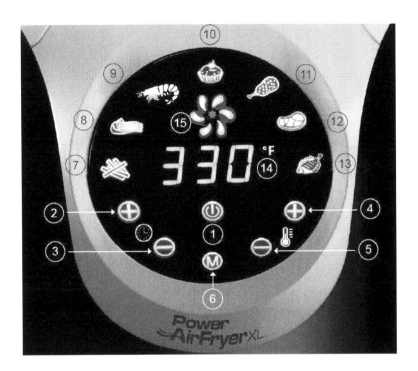

Selecting the Power Button (1) one time sets the appliance to a default temperature of 370°F, and the cooking time to 15 minutes. Selecting the Power Button a second time will start the cooking process. Pressing the power button during the cooking cycle will turn the unit off.

The + and – Buttons 2 & 3 enable to add or decrease cooking time, one minute at a time.

The + and – Buttons 4 & 5 enable to add or decrease cooking temperature, 10°F at a time.

Selecting the "M" Preset Button (6) enables you to scroll through the 7 popular food choices (4 in HF-509TS). These choices (Buttons 7 through 13) include **Fries**, **Chops** and other smaller cuts of meat, **Shrimp**, **Baked goods**, **Chicken**, **Steak**, and **Fish**.

The display 14 monitors the temperature and remaining cook time.

The spinning fan display (15) appears when the Fryer is turned on and for up to 20 seconds after it is turned off. A red, star-shaped LED appears in the center of the fan when the Unit is in Cook or Preheat mode.

If you want to experiment with the recipes given below, no need to choose a preset function. You can choose the time and temperature that suits your taste.

You may preheat the Fryer for more efficient cooking simply by selecting a cook time of 2 or 3 minutes and cook at the default or higher temperature. For preheating, you will need to insert the empty Fry Basket and Outer Basket into the Unit housing.

Place a baking tin or oven dish in the Fry Basket when baking a cake or quiche. A tin or dish is also suggested when cooking fragile or filled foods.

Estimating Nutritional Value

The nutritional value of the meals has been determined by simply adding up the values of each ingredient in the recipe based on the yield after cooking. The exact amount will vary depending on cooking temperature and time, ingredient mass density and bulk density, and the specific type of ingredient used.

Easy Appetizer/Snack Ideas

1. Fried Chicken

Preparation time: 2 h 10 min
Cooking time: 20 min
Servings: 6
Nutrition per serving: **335** Calories   Calories from Fat **90**

Ingredients
3 thighs - raw chicken with skin on (skin not eaten), medium (324 Calories, Caloric Ratio: Fat 49%, Protein 51%)
3 legs - raw chicken with skin on (skin not eaten), medium (534 Calories, Caloric Ratio: Fat 41%, Protein 59%)
2 cup white flour (910 Calories, Caloric Ratio: Carbohydrate 86%, Fat 2%, Protein 12%)
½ tablespoon black pepper (8 Calories, Caloric Ratio: Carbohydrate 81%, Fat 11%, Protein 8%)
½ tablespoon garlic powder (14 Calories, Caloric Ratio: Carbohydrate 84%, Fat 2%, Protein 14%)
½ teaspoon onion powder (4 Calories, Caloric Ratio: Carbohydrate 89%, Fat 3%, Protein 8%)
½ teaspoon poultry seasoning (2½ Calories, Caloric Ratio: Carbohydrate 72%, Fat 21%, Protein 7%)
3 teaspoons parsley (1 Calorie, Caloric Ratio: Carbohydrate 63%, Fat 18%, Protein 19%)

¼ teaspoon cumin (2 Calories, Caloric Ratio: Carbohydrate 34%, Fat 50%, Protein 16%)
¼ tablespoon paprika (5 Calories, Caloric Ratio: Carbohydrate 45%, Fat 38%, Protein 17%)
1 tablespoon olive oil (119 Calories, Caloric Ratio: Fat 100%)
1 cup buttermilk (Lowfat, Cultured) (98 Calories, Caloric Ratio: Carbohydrate 46%, Fat 19%, Protein 35%)
Optional: salt to taste (0 Calories, Caloric Ratio: Carbohydrate 100%)

Directions
Soak chicken in buttermilk in the fridge for 2 hours.
In a mixing bowl, combine the seasoning ingredients, mix well. Spread the flour in a separate bowl then add seasonings to the flour, and add salt. Mix well.
Roll chicken pieces in flour until all sides of them are completely coated with flour.
Place the chicken into the Fry Basket then pour olive oil.
Add the chicken pieces into your air fryer. Press the Preset Button then scroll to the Chicken Icon.
Press the Power Button & Air fry for 20 minutes and stir once at 360°F. Flip the chicken pieces every 5 minutes.
Serve and enjoy warm.

2. Delicious Chicken Fried in Egg and Flour

Preparation time: 3 h 15 min to 12 h 15 min
Cooking time: 20 min
Servings: 4
Nutrition per serving: **390** Calories   Calories from Fat **152**

Ingredients
2 chicken drumsticks with skin on (skin not eaten), medium (210 Calories, Caloric Ratio: Fat 48%, Protein 52%)
2 chicken thighs with skin on (skin not eaten), medium (304 Calories, Caloric Ratio: Fat 58%, Protein 42%)
1 tablespoon olive oil (119 Calories, Caloric Ratio: Fat 100%)
Marinade
2 cups buttermilk (Lowfat, Cultured) (196 Calories, Caloric Ratio: Carbohydrate 46%, Fat 19%, Protein 35%)
2 teaspoons black pepper (10 Calories, Caloric Ratio: Carbohydrate 81%, Fat 11%, Protein 8%)
1 teaspoon cayenne pepper (6 Calories, Caloric Ratio: Carbohydrate 42%, Fat 45%, Protein 13%)
1 tablespoon paprika (20 Calories, Caloric Ratio: Carbohydrate 45%, Fat 38%, Protein 17%)
2 teaspoons salt (0 Calories, Caloric Ratio: Carbohydrate 100%)

Seasoned Flour&Egg
1 cup all purpose flour (400 Calories, Caloric Ratio: Carbohydrate 88%, Protein 12%). Add some additional flour if needed to dress the chicken.
4 eggs, medium (260 Calories, Caloric Ratio: Carbohydrate 2%, Fat 63%, Protein 35%)
1 tablespoon baking powder (4 Calories, Caloric Ratio: Carbohydrate 99%, Protein 1%)
1 tablespoon garlic powder (28 Calories, Caloric Ratio: Carbohydrate 84%, Fat 2%, Protein 14%)
Optional: salt to taste (approx. ½ teaspoon)

Directions
Rinse chicken pieces thoroughly and remove the fat residue. In a separate bowl, combine black and cayenne pepper, paprika and salt, mix well. Then toss chicken pieces and season with the mixture.
Pour buttermilk over the chicken, and then stir until all pieces are completely coated with the mixture. Refrigerate for 3 to 12 hours.
Preheat your Air Fryer to 350°F.
Crack eggs then place in a deep plate. In another bowl, combine flour, baking powder, garlic powder, and salt. Dredge each piece of the chicken removed from the buttermilk through the seasoned flour mixture, then jiggle it gently under the egg and flip, then put back into the flour mixture again. You may repeat this entire process 2 or even 3 times.
Shake off any excess flour and transfer 4 chicken pieces onto the bottom of the Fry Basket then spray it lightly with oil and place the Basket into your Air Fryer. Put the chicken pieces in the Basket skin side up first, and leave them uncovered in order to prevent the skin from sticking to the basket when flipping the chicken.
Air fry for 10 minutes, pull out the Basket Assembly, turn chicken pieces over, and Air fry for another 10 minutes.
Serve and enjoy warm.

3. Dijon Lime Chicken

Preparation time: 10 minutes
Cooking time: 10 minutes
Servings: 8
Nutrition per serving: **97** Calories   Calories from Fat **40**

Ingredients
8 chicken drumsticks with skin on (skin not eaten), medium (576 Calories, Caloric Ratio: Fat 31%, Protein 69%)
1 lime, juiced (10 Calories, Caloric Ratio: Carbohydrate 91%, Fat 2%, Protein 7%)
1 tablespoon light mayonnaise (10 Calories, Caloric Ratio: Carbohydrate 11%, Fat 89%)
¾ teaspoon black pepper (5 Calories, Caloric Ratio: Carbohydrate 81%, Fat 11%, Protein 8%)
1 clove garlic, chopped (4 Calories, Caloric Ratio: Carbohydrate 85%, Fat 3%, Protein 12%)
3 tablespoons Dijon mustard (36 Calories, Caloric Ratio: Carbohydrate 42%, Fat 37%, Protein 21%)
1 teaspoon parsley, dried (1 Calorie, Caloric Ratio: Carbohydrate 67%, Fat 13%, Protein 20%)
1 tablespoon olive oil (119 Calories, Caloric Ratio: Fat 100%)
Optional: salt to taste

Directions

Preheat your Air Fryer to 375°F.

During this time, remove the skin of the chicken then season the chicken with salt and place in a container.

Place the Dijon mustard with lime juice in a separate bowl, add pepper, parsley, and garlic then mix well.

Pour the lime mixture over the chicken drumsticks, and then stir until all of the pieces are completely coated with the mixture.

Marinate the chicken for about 10 to 15 minutes and then discard marinade.

Place the chicken into the Fry Basket then spray it lightly with oil and place the Basket into your Air Fryer.

Air fry for 5 minutes, flip the drumsticks and fry for another 5 minutes.

Serve with the mayo and enjoy warm.

4. Chicken Wings

Preparation time: 5 minutes
Cooking time: 20 minutes
Servings: 3
Nutrition per serving: **267** Calories   Calories from Fat **136**

Ingredients
6 chicken wings (432 Calories, Caloric Ratio: Fat 65%, Protein 35%)
1 cup sweet and sour sauce / or other sauce of your choice (230 Calories, Caloric Ratio: Carbohydrate 98%, Protein 2%)
1 clove garlic, minced (4 Calories, Caloric Ratio: Carbohydrate 85%, Fat 3%, Protein 12%)
2 teaspoons chili powder (16 Calories, Caloric Ratio: Carbohydrate 42%, Fat 45%, Protein 13%)
1 tablespoon olive oil (119 Calories, Caloric Ratio: Fat 100%)
Optional: salt and black pepper to taste

Directions
Preheat your Air Fryer to 400°F.
During this time, remove the skin of the chicken then season the chicken with salt and pepper in a container.
Combine the garlic, chili powder, sauce in a separate bowl then mix. Pour the mixture over the chicken wings, and then stir until all of the pieces are completely coated with the mixture.

Remove chicken from sauce then set the latter aside for a while.
Place the chicken into the Fry Basket, spray your Air Fryer with oil using cooking spray then place the Basket into the Fryer.
Air fry for 10 minutes then pour the remaining sauce over the chicken wings and fry for another 10 minutes.
Serve with any salad and enjoy warm.

5. Fried Breakfast Sausage

Preparation time: 2 minutes
Cooking time: 4 minutes
Servings: 3
Nutrition per serving: **186** Calories   Calories from Fat **148**

Ingredients
6 raw uncooked pork sausages (510 Calories, Caloric Ratio: Fat 79%, Protein 21%)
1 tablespoon chives, finely chopped (1 Calorie, Caloric Ratio: Carbohydrate 52%, Fat 20%, Protein 28%)
1 teaspoon fennel (7 Calories, Caloric Ratio: Carbohydrate 49%, Fat 36%, Protein 15%)
1 teaspoon olive oil (40 Calories, Caloric Ratio: Fat 100%)

Directions
Preheat your Air Fryer to 375°F.
During this time, prick sausages before they are cooking, which allows the fat inside them to drip out while Air frying.
Place the sausages into the Fry Basket making sure they don't touch each other. Otherwise please use a Double Layer Rack.
Spray your Air Fryer with oil using cooking spray then place the Basket or Rack into the Fryer.
Air fry for about 3 minutes then sprinkle chives and fennel over the sausages and Air fry for less than 30 seconds.

Serve with baked beans in tomato sauce and fried eggs, if desired. Enjoy warm!

6. Simple Sausage Patties

Preparation time: 5 minutes
Cooking time: 6 minutes
Servings: 5
Nutrition per serving: **260** Calories   Calories from Fat **191**

Ingredients
1 pound coarsely ground pork shoulder (1193 Calories, Caloric Ratio: Fat 73%, Protein 27%)
1 garlic clove, minced (4 Calories, Caloric Ratio: Carbohydrate 85%, Fat 3%, Protein 12%)
1 tablespoon ground sage, crumbled (6 Calories, Caloric Ratio: Carbohydrate 58%, Fat 34%, Protein 8%)
¾ teaspoon dried thyme (3 Calories, Caloric Ratio: Carbohydrate 70%, Fat 23%, Protein 7%)
½ teaspoon dried fennel, crushed (3 Calories, Caloric Ratio: Carbohydrate 49%, Fat 36%, Protein 15%)
Pinch of ground nutmeg (¾ Calorie, Caloric Ratio: Carbohydrate 38%, Fat 58%, Protein 4%)
½ to 1½ teaspoons coarse salt (0 Calories, Caloric Ratio: Carbohydrate 100%)
½ teaspoon black pepper (2½ Calories, Caloric Ratio: Carbohydrate 81%, Fat 11%, Protein 8%)

1 egg white, large (17 Calories, Caloric Ratio: Carbohydrate 5%, Fat 3%, Protein 92%)
2 teaspoons vegetable oil (80 Calories, Caloric Ratio: Fat 100%)
Optional: salt to taste

Directions
Preheat your Air Fryer to 375°F.
In a mixing bowl, combine pork, garlic, sage, thyme, fennel, nutmeg, salt, and pepper then mix them until even. Add the egg white and stir thoroughly to combine.
With lightly oiled hands, divide the mixture into about 8-10 portions and shape each portion into a 2-inch disk. Place the disks into the Fry Basket. Spray your Air Fryer with oil using cooking spray then place the Basket into your Air Fryer.
Air fry for about 6 minutes.
Sprinkle with a little salt and serve warm. Decorate your patties with the lime wedges, rings of chopped red pepper, green chutney.

7. Meatballs with Yogurt

Preparation time: 10 minutes
Cooking time: 8 minutes
Servings: 4
Nutrition per serving: **447** Calories   Calories from Fat **232**

Ingredients:
1lbs ground beef (1255 Calories, Caloric Ratio: Fat 62%, Protein 38%)
1 tablespoon tabasco (0 Calories, Caloric Ratio: Carbohydrate 100%)
2 tablespoons Worcester sauce (0 Calories, Caloric Ratio: Carbohydrate 100%)
1 tablespoon lemon juice (12 Calories, Caloric Ratio: Carbohydrate 93%, Protein 7%)
½ cup brown sugar (270 Calories, Caloric Ratio: Carbohydrate 100%)
1 tablespoon ginger powder (6 Calories, Caloric Ratio: Carbohydrate 85%, Fat 8%, Protein 7%)
1 teaspoon ground cumin (2 Calories, Caloric Ratio: Carbohydrate 34%, Fat 50%, Protein 16%)
1 tablespoon parsley, finely chopped (1 Calorie, Caloric Ratio: Carbohydrate 63%, Fat 18%, Protein 19%)
1 teaspoon olive oil (40 Calories, Caloric Ratio: Fat 100%)
Yogurt
½ cup 0% greek yogurt (65 Calories, Caloric Ratio: Carbohydrate 28%, Protein 72%)

¼ cup sour cream (123 Calories, Caloric Ratio: Carbohydrate 8%, Fat 86%, Protein 6%)
2 tablespoons buttermilk (Lowfat) (12 Calories, Caloric Ratio: Carbohydrate 46%, Fat 19%, Protein 35%)

Directions
Preheat your Air Fryer to 390°F.
In a mixing bowl, combine all ingredients for the meatballs, mix them until even.
Roll meatballs with lightly oiled hands. With a light rolling motion form medium sized balls then place them into the Fry Basket. Spray your Air Fryer with oil using cooking spray then place the Basket into the Fryer.
Air fry for about 8 minutes.
When you've finished the meatballs, add yogurt, sour cream, and buttermilk into a mixing bowl then combine well.
Serve meatballs bathed in a warm yogurt sauce. Toss a few cucumber slices.

8. Banana Peppers with Salami Roll Ups

Preparation time: 5 minutes
Cooking time: 8 minutes
Servings: 3
Nutrition per serving: **460** Calories   Calories from Fat **328**

Ingredients
6 large banana peppers (120 Calories, Caloric Ratio: Carbohydrate 71%, Fat 14%, Protein 15%)
½ cup shredded cheddar cheese (455 Calories, Caloric Ratio: Carbohydrate 1%, Fat 72%, Protein 27%)
6 thin salami slices (210 Calories, Caloric Ratio: Carbohydrate 3%, Fat 74%, Protein 23%)
2 cups sliced avocados (470 Calories, Caloric Ratio: Carbohydrate 19%, Fat 77%, Protein 4%)
¼ cup chopped celery (3 Calories, Caloric Ratio: Carbohydrate 76%, Fat 10%, Protein 14%)
1 teaspoon ground oregano (9 Calories, Caloric Ratio: Carbohydrate 63%, Fat 28%, Protein 9%)
1 tablespoon olive oil (119 Calories, Caloric Ratio: Fat 100%)
Optional: salt and pepper to taste

Directions
Preheat your Air Fryer to 400°F.

Cut off the stem of peppers, and remove ribs and seeds. Cut a slit on one side of each pepper then set aside for a while.
Season cheese with celery, oregano, salt, and pepper then mix well. Place 1-2 spoons full of the cheese mixture into each banana pepper then add one slice of avocado in it. Wrap the peppers with salami slices then use toothpicks to seal.
Grease the Fry Basket with cooking spray, place the roll ups into it then place the Basket into the Fryer.
Air fry for about 5 to 8 minutes.
Serve and enjoy warm.

9. Mozzarella Sticks

Preparation time: 5 minutes
Cooking time: 10 minutes
Servings: 3
Nutrition per serving: **569** Calories   Calories from Fat **285**

Ingredients
12 mozzarella cheese sticks, Trader Joe's (840 Calories, Caloric Ratio: Fat 69%, Protein 31%)
2 eggs, medium (130 Calories, Caloric Ratio: Carbohydrate 2%, Fat 63%, Protein 35%)
¼ cup whole milk (37 Calories, Caloric Ratio: Carbohydrate 30%, Fat 49%, Protein 21%)
¼ cup all-purpose flour (100 Calories, Caloric Ratio: Carbohydrate 88%, Protein 12%)
1 cup bread crumbs, plain (480 Calories, Caloric Ratio: Carbohydrate 74%, Fat 12%, Protein 14%)
1 tablespoon olive oil (119 Calories, Caloric Ratio: Fat 100%)
pinch of salt (0 Calories, Caloric Ratio: Carbohydrate 100%)

Directions
Crack eggs then place in a deep plate and mix with milk. In two separate bowls, combine flour and salt, and blend bread crumbs.

Coat each mozzarella stick in flour in one at a time, then in the egg mixture, and finally in the bread crumbs.
Store coated sticks in the fridge for a couple of hours.
Place the sticks into the Fry Basket making sure they don't touch each other. Otherwise please use a Double Layer Rack.
Spray your Air Fryer with oil using cooking spray then place the Basket or Rack into your Air Fryer.
Air fry for about 10 minutes at 375°F.
Serve and enjoy warm.

10. Fish Sticks

Preparation time: 5 minutes
Cooking time: 12 minutes
Servings: 4
Nutrition per serving: **330** Calories   Calories from Fat **55**

Ingredients
1 lbs cod fillets, cut into 1-inch strips (360 Calories, Caloric Ratio: Fat 6%, Protein 94%)
2 eggs, medium (130 Calories, Caloric Ratio: Carbohydrate 2%, Fat 63%, Protein 35%)
½ cup all-purpose flour (200 Calories, Caloric Ratio: Carbohydrate 88%, Protein 12%)
1 cup bread crumbs, plain (480 Calories, Caloric Ratio: Carbohydrate 74%, Fat 12%, Protein 14%)
¼ cup whole milk (37 Calories, Caloric Ratio: Carbohydrate 30%, Fat 49%, Protein 21%)
½ teaspoon lemon pepper seasoning (0 Calories, Caloric Ratio: Carbohydrate 100%)
1 tablespoon olive oil (119 Calories, Caloric Ratio: Fat 100%)
Optional: salt to taste, approx. ½ teaspoon

Directions

Crack eggs then place in a shallow bowl and mix with milk. In two separate bowls, combine flour and salt, and mix bread crumbs and seasonings.

Roll fish in flour until all sides of the strips are completely coated with flour then shake off excess. Dip fish sticks into the egg mixture then roll in the crumb mixture. Make sure the coatings adhere to the stick surface by patting fish.

Place the sticks into the Fry Basket making sure they don't touch each other. Otherwise please use a Double Layer Rack. Spray your Air Fryer with oil using cooking spray then place the Basket or Rack into the Fryer.

Scroll the Fish Icon and air fry for about 10 to 12 minutes at 350°F. Flip once half way through cooking.

Serve with tartar sauce, potato chips, and lemon wedges, if desired.

11. Cinnamon Apple Chips

Preparation time: 5 minutes
Cooking time: 10 minutes
Servings: 3
Nutrition per serving: **90** Calories   Calories from Fat **2**

Ingredients
3 apples, medium (ideally, use Honey Crisp or Granny Smith) (210 Calories, Caloric Ratio: Carbohydrate 96%, Fat 3%, Protein 1%)
2 teaspoon ground cinnamon (10 Calories, Caloric Ratio: Carbohydrate 100%)
1 tablespoon sugar (48 Calories, Caloric Ratio: Carbohydrate 100%)
pinch of salt (0 Calories, Caloric Ratio: Carbohydrate 100%)

Directions
Preheat your Air Fryer to 400°F.
Wash, peel, core, and thinly slice apples then place slices onto the Double Layer Rack making sure they don't touch each other. Set the Rack aside for a while.
In a separate bowl, mix cinnamon, sugar, and salt then sprinkle the resulting powder evenly over the apple. Place the Rack into your Air Fryer.
Air fry for about 8 to 10 minutes, until the slices are golden brown. Turn them over once half way through cooking.

Remove from the Fryer then place in a bowl and cool to room temperature. Serve and enjoy.
The chips can be stored at room temperature in an airtight container for up to 1 week.

12. Sweet Potato Slices

Preparation time: 5 minutes
Cooking time: 15 minutes
Servings: 2
Nutrition per serving: **175** Calories   Calories from Fat **61**

Ingredients
2 sweet potatoes, large (220 Calories, Caloric Ratio: Carbohydrate 94%, Protein 6%)
1 teaspoon paprika (7 Calories, Caloric Ratio: Carbohydrate 45%, Fat 38%, Protein 17%)
½ teaspoon black pepper (2½ Calories, Caloric Ratio: Carbohydrate 81%, Fat 11%, Protein 8%)
1 tablespoon parsley, finely chopped (1 Calorie, Caloric Ratio: Carbohydrate 63%, Fat 18%, Protein 19%)
1 tablespoon olive oil (119 Calories, Caloric Ratio: Fat 100%)
Optional: salt to taste

Directions
Preheat your Air Fryer to 350°F.
Wash, peel, and cut potatoes in thin (approx. ¼ in.) slices.

In a small bowl, mix paprika, pepper, and salt. Toss the slices and cover well with spices. Arrange potatoes in a single layer in the Fry Basket or in the Double Layer Rack.

Spray your Air Fryer with olive oil using cooking spray then place the Basket or Rack into the Fryer.

Air fry for about 15 minutes. Turn the slices over once half way through cooking. Cook until both sides are crisp. Frying time will vary, depending on the slice thickness.

Sprinkle with chopped parsley for garnish and serve warm. Decorate with freshly grated Swiss cheese, if desired.

13. Parmesan Crumbed Fish

Preparation time: 5 minutes
Cooking time: 7 minutes
Servings: 2
Nutrition per serving: **502** Calories   Calories from Fat **299**

Ingredients
2 white fish fillets (skin off, 5 oz each) (250 Calories, Caloric Ratio: Fat 20%, Protein 80%)
1 egg, medium (65 Calories, Caloric Ratio: Carbohydrate 2%, Fat 63%, Protein 35%)
½ cup breadcrumbs (140 Calories, Caloric Ratio: Carbohydrate 88%, Protein 12%)
1 tablespoon parsley, finely chopped (1 Calorie, Caloric Ratio: Carbohydrate 63%, Fat 18%, Protein 19%)
2 tablespoons parmesan, grated (44 Calorie, Caloric Ratio: Carbohydrate 4%, Fat 58%, Protein 38%)
1 clove garlic, minced (4 Calories, Caloric Ratio: Carbohydrate 85%, Fat 3%, Protein 12%)
1 lemon (20 Calorie, Caloric Ratio: Carbohydrate 84%, Fat 6%, Protein 10%)
4 tablespoons vegetable oil (480 Calories, Caloric Ratio: Fat 100%)
pinch of salt (0 Calories, Caloric Ratio: Carbohydrate 100%)

Directions

Preheat your Air Fryer to 375°F.

In a bowl, combine breadcrumbs, parmesan, garlic, salt, and pour 3 tablespoons of vegetable oil then mix well to combine, until the mixture gets crumbly.

In a mixing bowl, crack an egg then whisk until it gets light and fluffy.

Add the fish fillets into the egg mixture first and then roll it in the breadcrumbs. Place fish fillets in the egg mixture then roll in the crumb mixture, until all sides of the fillets are completely coated then shake off excess. Make sure the breadcrumbs really adhere to the fillet surface.

Place the crumbed fish fillets into the Fry Basket. Spray your Air Fryer with a tablespoon of olive oil using cooking spray then place the Basket into the Fryer.

Air fry for about 5 to 7 minutes.

Serve warm, with some of the cooking coulis and mixed greens, if desired.

14. Salmon Burgers

Preparation time: 10 minutes
Cooking time: 6 minutes
Servings: 6
Nutrition per serving: **430** Calories   Calories from Fat **123**

Ingredients
1 (16 oz) can salmon, drained and flaked (660 Calories, Caloric Ratio: Fat 38%, Protein 62%)
2 cups flaked salmon (380 Calories, Caloric Ratio: Fat 29%, Protein 71%)
1 cup breadcrumbs (280 Calories, Caloric Ratio: Carbohydrate 88%, Protein 12%)
2 eggs, medium (130 Calories, Caloric Ratio: Carbohydrate 2%, Fat 63%, Protein 35%)
1 tablespoon parsley, finely chopped (1 Calorie, Caloric Ratio: Carbohydrate 63%, Fat 18%, Protein 19%)
3 tablespoons lemon juice (canned or bottled) (9 Calories, Caloric Ratio: Carbohydrate 83%, Fat 12%, Protein 5%)

2 tablespoons onion, finely chopped (8 Calories, Caloric Ratio: Carbohydrate 92%, Fat 2%, Protein 6%)
½ teaspoon dried basil (2 Calories, Caloric Ratio: Carbohydrate 73%, Fat 13%, Protein 14%)
¼ teaspoon garlic salt (0 Calories, Caloric Ratio: Carbohydrate 100%)
1 tablespoon light mayonnaise (10 Calories, Caloric Ratio: Carbohydrate 11%, Fat 89%)
1 tablespoon olive oil (119 Calories, Caloric Ratio: Fat 100%)
6 hamburger buns, split (960 Calories, Caloric Ratio: Carbohydrate 70%, Fat 17%, Protein 13%)
6 lettuce leaves (15 Calories, Caloric Ratio: Carbohydrate 67%, Protein 33%)

Directions
Preheat your Air Fryer to 350°F.
In a bowl, crack eggs and whisk until fluffy, then add and mix salmon, parsley, onion, breadcrumbs, 2 tablespoons of lemon juice, approx. 1/2 teaspoon of basil (keep a pinch for a sauce), and garlic salt. Form into 6 flat burger patties, approx. ½ inch thick.
Place the burger patties into the Fry Basket. Spray your Air Fryer with a tablespoon of olive oil using cooking spray then place the Basket into the Fryer.
Air fry for about 5 to 6 minutes, until nicely browned.
In a separate bowl, mix mayonnaise, 1 tablespoon of lemon juice and a pinch of basil. Use this as a sauce for your burgers.
Top each burger with sauce and lettuce leaves, serve on hamburger buns.

15. Coconut Shrimp Skewers

Preparation time: 10 minutes & marinating time
Cooking time: 10 minutes
Servings: 4
Nutrition per serving: Calories **426**   Calories from Fat **183**

Ingredients
1½ lbs shrimp, peeled and deveined (980 Calories, Caloric Ratio: Carbohydrate 4%, Fat 15%, Protein 81%)
½ cup parmesan cheese, grated (215 Calories, Caloric Ratio: Carbohydrate 4%, Fat 58%, Protein 38%)
¼ cup coconut, shredded (71 Calories, Caloric Ratio: Carbohydrate 18%, Fat 79%, Protein 3%)
1 clove garlic, minced (4 Calories, Caloric Ratio: Carbohydrate 85%, Fat 3%, Protein 12%)
4 tablespoons fresh basil leaves, chopped (2 Calories, Caloric Ratio: Carbohydrate 57%, Fat 19%, Protein 24%)

1 tablespoon ginger root (fresh), minced (6 Calories, Caloric Ratio: Carbohydrate 85%, Fat 8%, Protein 7%)
4 tablespoons fresh lime juice (16 Calories, Caloric Ratio: Carbohydrate 91%, Fat 2%, Protein 7%)
3 tablespoons olive oil (357 Calories, Caloric Ratio: Fat 100%)
2 tablespoons coconut milk (53 Calories, Caloric Ratio: Carbohydrate 8%, Fat 89%, Protein 3%)
Optional: sea salt and fresh pepper to taste
8 wooden skewers

Directions
In a bowl, combine ginger, garlic, basil, parmesan cheese, 2 tablespoons of lime juice, coconut, 2 tablespoons of olive oil, pepper, and salt. Add shrimp, tossing to coat, then cover the bowl, chill it, and let shrimp marinate for at least 1 to several hours.
Thereafter, preheat your Air Fryer to 320°F.
Now use the skewers to thread the shrimp. Place the shrimp skewers into the Fry Basket. Spray your Air Fryer with a tablespoon of olive oil using cooking spray then place the Basket into the Fryer.
Air fry for about 10 minutes.
Arrange shrimp skewers on a serving plate and sprinkle evenly with 2 tablespoons of lime juice, and coconut milk. Serve warm.

Vegetarian Appetizer/Snack

16. Kale Chips

Preparation time: 5 minutes
Cooking time: 3 minutes
Servings: 2
Nutrition per serving: Calories **102**   Calories from Fat **65**

Ingredients
1 bunch kale (6 oz with stem and 10 leaves intact, approx. 4 oz in leaves) (56 Calories, Caloric Ratio: Carbohydrate 71%, Fat 12%, Protein 17%)
1 teaspoon garlic powder (9 Calories, Caloric Ratio: Carbohydrate 84%, Fat 2%, Protein 14%)
1 tablespoon soy sauce (8 Calories, Caloric Ratio: Carbohydrate 54%, Fat 1%, Protein 45%)
1 teaspoon chili powder (8 Calories, Caloric Ratio: Carbohydrate 42%, Fat 45%, Protein 13%)
½ teaspoon onion powder (4 Calories, Caloric Ratio: Carbohydrate 89%, Fat 3%, Protein 8%)
1 tablespoon olive oil (119 Calories, Caloric Ratio: Fat 100%)

Directions
Remove leaves from the stem using a knife or kitchen shears then tear the kale leaves into large pieces. Rinse thoroughly and dry them. Drizzle kale with olive oil and sprinkle with seasoning salt.
Place the leaves into a large bowl then sprinkle the spices & seasonings over them and toss to combine.
Preheat your Air Fryer to 390°F.
Arrange the leaves in a single layer in the Fry Basket making sure they don't touch each other. Otherwise please use a Double Layer Rack. Spray your Air Fryer with oil using cooking spray then place the Basket or Rack into the Fryer.
Air fry for about 2 to 3 minutes. Turn the leaves over once half way through cooking.
When serving, add soy sauce, if desired. Enjoy your chips warm or chilled.

17. Swedish Bean Curd Meatballs

Preparation time: 10 minutes
Cooking time: 5 minutes
Servings: 2
Nutrition per serving: Calories **210**   Calories from Fat **110**

Ingredients
2 slices firm silken tofu (approx. 6 oz) (104 Calories, Caloric Ratio: Carbohydrate 15%, Fat 39%, Protein 46%)
½ cup vegetable broth (8 Calories, Caloric Ratio: Carbohydrate 100%)
¼ cup skim milk (22 Calories, Caloric Ratio: Carbohydrate 59%, Protein 41%)
¼ cup soy milk (32 Calories, Caloric Ratio: Carbohydrate 39%, Fat 31%, Protein 30%)
2 clove garlic, finely chopped (8 Calories, Caloric Ratio: Carbohydrate 85%, Fat 3%, Protein 12%)
4 tablespoons coconut flour (90 Calories, Caloric Ratio: Carbohydrate 56%, Fat 23%, Protein 21%)
4 tablespoons almond flour (170 Calories, Caloric Ratio: Carbohydrate 12%, Fat 75%, Protein 13%)
1 beet (approx. 2 inches in diameter), peeled & shredded (35 Calories, Caloric Ratio: Carbohydrate 85%, Fat 3%, Protein 12%)

2 teaspoons black pepper (10 Calories, Caloric Ratio: Carbohydrate 81%, Fat 11%, Protein 8%)
1 teaspoon salt (0 Calories, Caloric Ratio: Carbohydrate 100%)
1 tablespoon chia seeds, soaked (22 Calories, Caloric Ratio: Carbohydrate 38%, Fat 43%, Protein 19%)
2 teaspoons dried thyme (8 Calories, Caloric Ratio: Carbohydrate 70%, Fat 23%, Protein 7%)
1 tablespoon olive oil (119 Calories, Caloric Ratio: Fat 100%)

Directions
Preheat your Air Fryer to 350°F.
In a large bowl, combine tofu, garlic, beet, thyme, salt, and pepper then mix well and add the coconut flour, almond flour, and vegetable broth. Mash adding chia seeds and pouring milk until the mixture is close to the finished sticky texture you'd like. Form into medium size balls, nearly 1 to 1½ inches in diameter. If the mixture is too dry, simply add some skim/soy milk.
Arrange the balls in a single layer in the Fry Basket making sure they don't touch each other. Spray your Air Fryer with oil using cooking spray then place the Basket or Rack into the Fryer.
Air fry for about 4 to 5 minutes.
Serve over noodles, if desired.

18. Veggie Vegetable Fries

Preparation time: 5 minutes
Cooking time: 15 minutes
Servings: 4
Nutrition per serving: Calories **144**   Calories from Fat **62**

Ingredients
2 sweet potatoes, large (220 Calories, Caloric Ratio: Carbohydrate 94%, Protein 6%)
2 zucchini, medium (62 Calories, Caloric Ratio: Carbohydrate 75%, Fat 9%, Protein 16%)
2 carrots, medium (50 Calories, Caloric Ratio: Carbohydrate 90%, Fat 5%, Protein 5%)
1 teaspoon dried thyme (4 Calories, Caloric Ratio: Carbohydrate 70%, Fat 23%, Protein 7%)
½ teaspoon dried basil (2 Calories, Caloric Ratio: Carbohydrate 73%, Fat 13%, Protein 14%)
2 tablespoons olive oil (238 Calories, Caloric Ratio: Fat 100%)
Optional: salt and pepper to taste

Directions
Preheat your Air Fryer to 355°F.
Wash, peel, and cut potatoes, carrots, and zucchini into chunky chips shape.
Place them in the Fry Basket then spray your Air Fryer with oil using cooking spray and place the Basket into the Fryer.

Air fry for about 18 to 20 minutes. Give them the shake twice through cooking thus distributing the heat more evenly.
Once the fries are done, place them in a bowl and season with thyme, basil, salt & pepper. Serve and enjoy your fries warm or chilled.

19. Honey Brussells Sprouts with Pecans

Preparation time: 10 minutes
Cooking time: 14 minutes
Servings: 4
Nutrition per serving: Calories **180**   Calories from Fat **132**

Ingredients
½ lbs fresh Brussels sprouts (98 Calories, Caloric Ratio: Carbohydrate 74%, Fat 6%, Protein 20%)
1 tablespoon butter (102 Calories, Caloric Ratio: Fat 99%, Protein 1%)
1 tablespoon honey (64 Calories, Caloric Ratio: Carbohydrate 100%)
¼ cup pecans, chopped (205 Calories, Caloric Ratio: Carbohydrate 7%, Fat 88%, Protein 5%)
2 tablespoon olive oil (238 Calories, Caloric Ratio: Fat 100%)
1 tablespoon balsamic vinegar (13 Calories, Caloric Ratio: Carbohydrate 100%)
Optional: kosher salt and ground pepper to taste

Directions

Preheat your Air Fryer to 355°F.
To roast pecans, put them onto a small cookie sheet/paper holder, move it in the Fry Basket then place into the Fryer. Air fry for 4 minutes. Give the shake once half way through cooking. Remove the pecans holder then set aside for a while. Slice Brussels sprouts in half lengthwise. In a bowl, toss together the sprouts, 1 tablespoon oil, vinegar, salt, and pepper. Gently stir, but don't break sprouts apart. Place them in the Fry Basket then spray your Air Fryer with the remaining oil using cooking spray and place the Basket into the Fryer. Air fry for about 8 to 10 minutes 400°F, until crispy and browned, shaking after 4 minutes and then after 7 minutes. Don't burn!
In the meantime, place butter and honey into a small saucepan then render them gently over low heat until they are combined.
Remove the sprouts from the Fry Basket, place in a deep plate then pour on the honey butter, top with the pecans, and very gently toss until well coated.
Serve slightly warm on a serving platter.

20. Gujiya

Preparation time: 20 min
Cooking time: 15 min
Servings: 3
Nutrition per serving: Calories **277**   Calories from Fat **100**

Ingredients
1 cup refined flour (455 Calories, Caloric Ratio: Carbohydrate 86%, Fat 2%, Protein 12%)
1 tablespoon ghee oil (130 Calories, Caloric Ratio: Fat 100%)
¼ lbs khoua, grated
1 tablespoon cashew nut, chopped (55 Calories, Caloric Ratio: Carbohydrate 22%, Fat 66%, Protein 12%)
⅓ oz raisins (8 Calories, Caloric Ratio: Carbohydrate 97%, Protein 3%)
2½ teaspoons ground cardamom (15 Calories, Caloric Ratio: Carbohydrate 70%, Fat 18%, Protein 12%)
1 tablespoon sugar (48 Calories, Caloric Ratio: Carbohydrate 100%)
1 tablespoon olive oil (119 Calories, Caloric Ratio: Fat 100%)

Directions

Preheat your Air Fryer to 355°F.

In a bowl, add the flour and ghee then rub with your palm. Add water and knead a stiff dough. Cut the dough into equal portions, shape into small balls, and keep aside for 10-15 minutes.

In a separate bowl, mix khoua, nut, raisins, cardamom, and sugar and make the gujiya filling.

Roll each ball with the rolling pin into thin rounds (of soup bowl diameter) then spread a tablespoon of the filling on one-half of them. Brush the edges of the rolled out dough with water, press the ends and seal the edges with your finger.

Place the gujiya in the Fry Basket then spray your Air Fryer with oil using cooking spray and place the Basket into the Fryer.

Air fry for about 12 to 15 minutes, until golden brown. Flip once half way through cooking.

Serve and enjoy your gujiya warm.

Lunch/Dinner Ideas

21. Chicken and Zucchini Ranch Meatballs with Potatoes

Preparation time: 10 min
Cooking time: 12 min
Servings: 3
Nutrition per serving: **827** Calories   Calories from Fat **257**

Ingredients
1 lbs chicken mince (1075 Calories, Caloric Ratio: Fat 45%, Protein 55%)

½ lbs potatoes (190 Calories, Caloric Ratio: Carbohydrate 91%, Fat 1%, Protein 8%)
1 tablespoon barbecue sauce (12 Calories, Caloric Ratio: Carbohydrate 68%, Fat 22%, Protein 10%)
1 cup breadcrumbs (280 Calories, Caloric Ratio: Carbohydrate 88%, Protein 12%)
1 zucchini, medium (31 Calories, Caloric Ratio: Carbohydrate 75%, Fat 9%, Protein 16%)
1 egg, medium (65 Calories, Caloric Ratio: Carbohydrate 2%, Fat 63%, Protein 35%)
1/4 cup fresh chives, finely chopped (3 Calories, Caloric Ratio: Carbohydrate 52%, Fat 20%, Protein 28%)
2 tablespoons olive oil (238 Calories, Caloric Ratio: Fat 100%)
Optional: salt to taste

Ranch Dipping Sauce
0.2 lbs Danish blue cheese, crumbled (330 Calories, Caloric Ratio: Fat 82%, Protein 18%)
1/3 cup light mayonnaise (70 Calories, Caloric Ratio: Carbohydrate 11%, Fat 89%)
1/3 cup sour cream (160 Calories, Caloric Ratio: Carbohydrate 8%, Fat 86%, Protein 6%)
1/4 cup buttermilk (Lowfat, Cultured) (25 Calories, Caloric Ratio: Carbohydrate 46%, Fat 19%, Protein 35%)

Direction
Preheat your Air Fryer to 350°F.
Peel zucchini then cut it into thin slices. Clean and cube potatoes. Set the slices and cubes aside for a while.
In a mixing bowl, add the blue cheese, sour cream, and mayo. Mix well then add buttermilk. Mix until smooth then set aside for a while.
In a separate bowl, place chicken mince, breadcrumbs, barbecue sauce, chives. Crack an egg then place in the bowl. Mix well and season with salt.
Shape the mixture into 10 to 12 balls.
Take each zucchini slice and wrap around the meatball. Seal the edge using a toothpick.

Transfer the meatballs onto the bottom of the Fry Basket, add potatoes then spray them with oil and place the Basket into your Air Fryer. Air fry for 8 to 10 minutes.

Once the meatballs are done, remove them from the Basket then roll the meatballs into the dipping sauce.

Place the meatballs back into the Air Fryer. Air fry just for a couple of minutes at 350°F.

Serve the meatballs and potatoes warm with greens and the dipping sauce you made.

22. Turkey Meatballs with Tomato Gravy

Preparation time: 15 minutes
Cooking time: 30 minutes
Servings: 6
Nutrition per serving: **187** Calories   Calories from Fat **38**

Ingredients
Meatballs
1 lbs extra lean (99%) ground turkey (Jennie-O) (480 Calories, Caloric Ratio: Fat 11%, Protein 89%)
1 clove garlic, minced (4 Calories, Caloric Ratio: Carbohydrate 85%%, Fat 3%, Protein 12%)
1 teaspoon lemon juice (4 Calories, Caloric Ratio: Carbohydrate 93%, Protein 7%)
1 teaspoon chili powder (8 Calories, Caloric Ratio: Carbohydrate 42%, Fat 45%, Protein 13%)
3/4 teaspoon paprika (5 Calories, Caloric Ratio: Carbohydrate 45%, Fat 38%, Protein 17%)
1 teaspoon plain yogurt (3 Calories, Caloric Ratio: Carbohydrate 45%, Fat 22%, Protein 33%)
⅓ cup whole wheat breadcrumbs (150 Calories, Caloric Ratio: Carbohydrate 73%, Fat 12%, Protein 15%)
1 egg white, large (17 Calories, Caloric Ratio: Carbohydrate 5%, Fat 3%, Protein 92%)
½ teaspoon salt (0 Calories, Caloric Ratio: Carbohydrate 100%)

¼ teaspoon ground black pepper (0 Calories, Caloric Ratio: Carbohydrate 100%)

Gravy

1 tablespoon olive oil (119 Calories, Caloric Ratio: Fat 100%)
2 cups onion, finely chopped (135 Calories, Caloric Ratio: Carbohydrate 92%, Fat 2%, Protein 6%)
2 teaspoons ginger root (fresh), finely grated (4 Calories, Caloric Ratio: Carbohydrate 85%, Fat 8%, Protein 7%)
1 teaspoon garlic, minced (4 Calories, Caloric Ratio: Carbohydrate 85%, Fat 3%, Protein 12%)
5 medium tomatoes, chopped (110 Calories, Caloric Ratio: Carbohydrate 74%, Fat 9%, Protein 17%)
1 tablespoon turmeric (ground) (24 Calories, Caloric Ratio: Carbohydrate 70%, Fat 23%, Protein 7%)
2 teaspoons coriander powder (5 Calories, Caloric Ratio: Carbohydrate 36%, Fat 50%, Protein 14%)
1 teaspoon cumin powder (8 Calories, Caloric Ratio: Carbohydrate 34%, Fat 50%, Protein 16%)
2 teaspoons chili powder (10 Calories, Caloric Ratio: Carbohydrate 30%, Fat 49%, Protein 21%)
2 teaspoons sugar (32 Calories, Caloric Ratio: Carbohydrate 100%)

Directions

Place ground turkey, garlic, lemon juice, chili, paprika, yogurt, breadcrumbs, egg white, salt, and pepper into a bowl and mix well. Shape the mixture into 10 to 12 balls then set them aside for a while.

Preheat your Air Fryer to 165°F. Transfer the meatballs into the Fry Basket then spray them with oil and place the Basket into your Air Fryer. Air fry for 20 minutes.

To make gravy, finely chop onion, place it into a frying pan then pour olive oil. Sauté over medium-high heat until golden brown. Add ginger and garlic then sauté for 1 minute. Add tomatoes and sauté until tender for approximately 5 minutes. Add remaining ingredients (turmeric, coriander, cumin, chili powders and sugar) into a bowl and mix well. Sauté for 5 minutes.

Once the gravy is ready, transfer meatballs to the frying pan coating with gravy then braise them for about 5 minutes. Keep in mind that it's hard to overcook the meatballs at this stage as they're sitting in liquid sauce. Alternatively, set the coated meatballs in your Air Fryer to 370°F for about 2 minutes until you're ready to serve them.
Serve warm with greens.

23. Spicy Party Meatballs in Tomato Sauce

Preparation time: 20 minutes
Cooking time: 25 minutes
Servings: 5
Nutrition per serving: **524** Calories   Calories from Fat **131**

Ingredients
1 lbs minced beef (1310 Calories, Caloric Ratio: Fat 33%, Protein 67%)
1 tablespoon tabasco (0 Calories, Caloric Ratio: Carbohydrate 100%)
½ teaspoon mustard (1½ Calories, Caloric Ratio: Carbohydrate 42%, Fat 37%, Protein 21%)
3 gingersnaps, crushed (400 Calories, Caloric Ratio: Carbohydrate 74%, Fat 21%, Protein 5%)
1 tablespoon Worcester sauce (0 Calories, Caloric Ratio: Carbohydrate 100%)
1 tablespoon lemon juice (12 Calories, Caloric Ratio: Carbohydrate 93%, Protein 7%)
Tomato Sauce
4 cups tomato puree, canned or fresh (380 Calories, Caloric Ratio: Carbohydrate 81%, Fat 4%, Protein 15%)
3 tablespoons white flour (84 Calories, Caloric Ratio: Carbohydrate 86%, Fat 2%, Protein 12%)
1 clove garlic, chopped (4 Calories, Caloric Ratio: Carbohydrate 85%, Fat 3%, Protein 12%)

½ tablespoon oregano (9 Calories, Caloric Ratio: Carbohydrate 63%, Fat 28%, Protein 9%)
½ tablespoon basil (¼ Calories, Caloric Ratio: Carbohydrate 57%, Fat 19%, Protein 24%)
2 bay leaves (0 Calories, Caloric Ratio: Carbohydrate 100%)
¼ bottle white wine (100 Calories, Caloric Ratio: Carbohydrate 12%, Protein 88%)
¼ cup brown sugar (135 Calories, Caloric Ratio: Carbohydrate 100%)
½ tablespoon salt (0 Calories, Caloric Ratio: Carbohydrate 100%)
1 large onion, chopped (63 Calories, Caloric Ratio: Carbohydrate 92%, Fat 2%, Protein 6%)
1 tablespoon olive oil (119 Calories, Caloric Ratio: Fat 100%)
parsley and cheese for garnishing

Directions
Preheat your Air Fryer to 370°F.
In a large mixing bowl, place tabasco, mustard, gingersnaps, Worcester sauce, lemon juice, and sugar then blend, until all is evenly mixed. Add the mince to the bowl and mix until smooth.
Roll meatballs with lightly oiled hands. With a light rolling motion form medium sized balls then place them into the Fry Basket. Spray your Air Fryer with oil using cooking spray then place the Basket into the Fryer.
Air fry for about 10 minutes.
To make a sauce, finely chop onion, place it into a frying pan then pour olive oil. Sauté over medium-high heat until the onions are clear. Add garlic then sauté for 1 minute.
Pour tomato puree into a sauce pan. Add flour, onions, and spices (oregano, basil, and some others, if you like) then lightly mix. Be sure the flour is mixed in without any lumps. Bring to a light boil and simmer for 3 minutes then lower the heat. Cooling will thicken the sauce. Add wine, sugar and bay leaves. Boil for a couple of minutes.
Once the sauce is ready, place the meatballs carefully in the sauce. Simmer for another 10 minutes. Alternatively, set the

coated meatballs in your Air Fryer to 370°F for about 3 minutes until you're ready to serve them.
Before serving, sprinkle with parsley and cheese.

24. Chicken Lasagna

Preparation time: 10 minutes
Cooking time: 5+1+ minutes
Servings: 4
Nutrition per serving: Calories **883**   Calories from Fat **417**

Ingredients
15 oz chicken sausage (735 Calories, Caloric Ratio: Carbohydrate 3%, Fat 54%, Protein 43%)
¼ cup chili sauce (80 Calories, Caloric Ratio: Carbohydrate 100%)
3 clove garlic, minced (12 Calories, Caloric Ratio: Carbohydrate 85%, Fat 3%, Protein 12%)
½ large onion, chopped (31 Calories, Caloric Ratio: Carbohydrate 92%, Fat 2%, Protein 6%)
1 can (28 oz) crushed tomatoes (252 Calories, Caloric Ratio: Carbohydrate 81%, Fat 7%, Protein 12%)
2 tablespoons parsley, finely chopped (2 Calorie, Caloric Ratio: Carbohydrate 63%, Fat 18%, Protein 19%)
2 tablespoons fresh basil leaves, chopped (1 Calorie, Caloric Ratio: Carbohydrate 57%, Fat 19%, Protein 24%)
1-2 large fresh lasagne pasta sheets (210 Calories, Caloric Ratio: Carbohydrate 82%, Fat 4%, Protein 14%)
2 teaspoons corn flour (55 Calories, Caloric Ratio: Carbohydrate 81%, Fat 8%, Protein 11%)

¼ cup whole milk (37 Calories, Caloric Ratio: Carbohydrate 30%, Fat 49%, Protein 21%)
4 cups mozzarella cheese, shredded (1364 Calories, Caloric Ratio: Carbohydrate 5%, Fat 60%, Protein 35%)
1 cup part skim ricotta cheese (320 Calories, Caloric Ratio: Carbohydrate 30%, Fat 45%, Protein 25%)
1 egg, large (74 Calories, Caloric Ratio: Carbohydrate 2%, Fat 63%, Protein 35%)
3 tablespoons olive oil (357 Calories, Caloric Ratio: Carbohydrate 5%, Fat 60%, Protein 35%)
Optional: salt and pepper to taste

Directions
Pour 2 tablespoons of olive oil in a pan (alternatively: corn oil, canola oil, or butter). Heat this over medium heat until hot then brown chicken with garlic, onion, and basil. Add chili sauce and tomatoes and cook the mince for several minutes.
In a microwaveable container, combine flour, milk, salt, and pepper and then whisk until incorporated. Microwave on HIGH for 1 minute. Remove from the oven and whisk well then heat for 1 more minute. Whisk and microwave for the third time. Just add extra milk if the sauce is too thick.
In a bowl, add the parmesan cheese, egg, ricotta cheese, and parsley. Mix well and set aside for a while.
Preheat your Air Fryer to 340°F.
Cover the base of a casserole that fits into your Air Fryer with half the mince filling mixture. Cut a piece of lasagne sheet to fit across the top of the mixture. Set this on and cover with half the sauce and some of the cheese mixture. Cover this layer with the rest of the mince mixture.
Cut another piece of the lasagne sheet and lay it across the top of the lasagna then cover with the rest of the sauce. Sprinkle the cheese mixture over the top of the lasagne.
Carefully set casserole into your Air Fryer Basket. Spray your Air Fryer with 1 tablespoon of olive oil using cooking spray then place the Basket into the Fryer.
Air fry for 20 minutes.
Serve hot.

25. Balsamic Chicken with Veggies

Preparation time: 10 minutes
Cooking time: 20 minutes
Servings: 4
Nutrition per serving: Calories **451**   Calories from Fat **239**

Ingredients
8 chicken thighs with skin on (skin not eaten), medium (1208 Calories, Caloric Ratio: Fat 58%, Protein 42%)
5 oz mushrooms, sliced (30 Calories, Caloric Ratio: Carbohydrate 52%, Fat 13%, Protein 35%)
1 medium red onion, diced (46 Calories, Caloric Ratio: Carbohydrate 90%, Fat 2%, Protein 8%)
10 medium spears asparagus (30 Calories, Caloric Ratio: Carbohydrate 69%, Fat 5%, Protein 26%)
½ cup baby carrots (35 Calories, Caloric Ratio: Carbohydrate 89%, Protein 11%)

1 cup broccoli, chopped (31 Calories, Caloric Ratio: Carbohydrate 70%, Fat 9%, Protein 21%)
8 oz cherry tomatoes (40 Calories, Caloric Ratio: Carbohydrate 74%, Fat 9%, Protein 17%)
¼ cup balsamic vinegar (52 Calories, Caloric Ratio: Carbohydrate 100%)
2 medium red bell peppers, diced (60 Calories, Caloric Ratio: Carbohydrate 89%, Protein 11%)
½ teaspoon sugar (8 Calories, Caloric Ratio: Carbohydrate 100%)
1½ tablespoons fresh rosemary (3 Calories, Caloric Ratio: Carbohydrate 56%, Fat 37%, Protein 7%)
2 cloves garlic, chopped (8 Calories, Caloric Ratio: Carbohydrate 85%, Fat 3%, Protein 12%)
½ tablespoon oregano (9 Calories, Caloric Ratio: Carbohydrate 63%, Fat 28%, Protein 9%)
1 teaspoon kosher salt (0 Calories, Caloric Ratio: Carbohydrate 100%)
1 tablespoon sage, ground (6 Calories, Caloric Ratio: Carbohydrate 58%, Fat 34%, Protein 8%)
2 tablespoons extra virgin olive oil (238 Calories, Caloric Ratio: Fat 100%)
Optional: fresh parsley and black pepper to taste

Directions
Preheat your Air Fryer to 400°F.
Sprinkle the chicken with salt, pepper, and parsley then rub them evenly.
Slice the baby carrots in half, chop asparagus. Place carrots, broccoli, asparagus and tomatoes in a large bowl, pour 1 tablespoon of oil. Add sage, oregano, rosemary, garlic, red pepper, sugar, vinegar, and mushrooms. Mix until well combined and arrange into the Fry Basket. Add the chicken thighs as well.
Spray your Air Fryer with 1 tablespoon of oil using cooking spray then place the Basket into the Fryer.
Air fry for about 20 minutes.
Serve warm. Top with freshly chopped parsley and served over rice, if desired.

26. Honey Chicken Wings

Preparation time: 15 minutes
Cooking time: 35 minutes
Servings: 4
Nutrition per serving: Calories **436**   Calories from Fat **227**

Ingredients
8 chicken wings (576 Calories, Caloric Ratio: Fat 65%, Protein 35%)
½ cup potato starch (320 Calories, Caloric Ratio: Carbohydrate 100%)
¼ cup honey (256 Calories, Caloric Ratio: Carbohydrate 100%)
¼ cup butter (408 Calories, Caloric Ratio: Fat 99%, Protein 1%)
4 tablespoons fresh garlic, minced (48 Calories, Caloric Ratio: Carbohydrate 85%, Fat 3%, Protein 12%)
2 teaspoons chili powder (16 Calories, Caloric Ratio: Carbohydrate 42%, Fat 45%, Protein 13%)
1 tablespoon olive oil (119 Calories, Caloric Ratio: Fat 100%)
½ teaspoon salt (0 Calories, Caloric Ratio: Carbohydrate 100%)

Directions
Preheat your Air Fryer to 380°F.
During this time, remove the skin of the chicken wings then season the chicken with salt in a container.

Combine the garlic, chili powder, sauce in a separate bowl then mix. Pour the mixture over the chicken wings, and then stir until all of the pieces are completely coated with the mixture.

Add potato starch in the container, making sure that all wings are well coated.

Place the chicken into the Fry Basket, spray your Air Fryer with oil using cooking spray then place the Basket into the Fryer.

Air fry for 25 minutes giving them the shake every 5 minutes through cooking thus distributing the heat more evenly.

After 25 minutes, set the temperature to 400°F, so that, after 5 to 10 minutes, they're really crispy.

In the meantime, melt the butter in a saucepan over medium heat until it foams then add garlic and sauté for 5 minutes.

Add the honey and salt then continue to simmer over low heat for about 20 minutes. Make sure to stir every few minutes that allows heating the sauce evenly and thoroughly without scorching.

Remove the wings from your Air Fryer and place on a serving platter then pour over the sauce, making sure that all pieces are coated.

Enjoy warm.

27. Garlic Parsley Potatoes

Preparation time: 10 minutes
Cooking time: 40 minutes
Servings: 2
Nutrition per serving: Calories **300**   Calories from Fat **120**

Ingredients
3 Idaho or russet potatoes (330 Calories, Caloric Ratio: Carbohydrate 90%, Protein 10%)
1 tablespoon garlic powder (28 Calories, Caloric Ratio: Carbohydrate 84%, Fat 2%, Protein 14%)
1 teaspoon parsley, dried (1 Calorie, Caloric Ratio: Carbohydrate 67%, Fat 13%, Protein 20%)
½ teaspoon black pepper (2 Calories, Caloric Ratio: Carbohydrate 81%, Fat 11%, Protein 8%)
1 teaspoon salt (0 Calories, Caloric Ratio: Carbohydrate 100%)
2 tablespoons olive oil (238 Calories, Caloric Ratio: Fat 100%)

Directions
Cut potatoes in half or quarters then place in a bowl. Pour 1 tablespoon of olive oil, add salt, pepper, and garlic then toss until the potatoes are well coated.

Transfer the potatoes onto the bottom of the Fry Basket and spread out into 1 layer then spray it lightly with 1 tablespoon of oil then place the Basket into your Air Fryer.
Air fry at 390°F for about 35 to 40 minutes.
Serve warm with fresh parsley and sour cream on top.

28. Potato Creamy Casserole Gratin

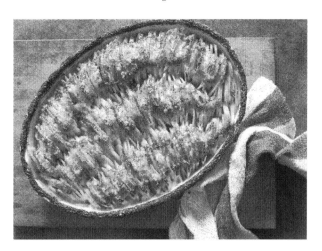

Preparation time: 15 minutes
Cooking time: 22 minutes
Servings: 6
Nutrition per serving: Calories **554**   Calories from Fat **335**

Ingredients
3 lbs russet potatoes, medium, peeled and sliced (1074 Calories, Caloric Ratio: Carbohydrate 92%, Fat 1%, Protein 7%)
2 cups heavy cream (1642 Calories, Caloric Ratio: Carbohydrate 3%, Fat 95%, Protein 2%)
1 tablespoon butter (102 Calories, Caloric Ratio: Fat 99%, Protein 1%)
2 cloves garlic, minced (8 Calories, Caloric Ratio: Carbohydrate 85%, Fat 3%, Protein 12%)
1 tablespoon dried thyme leaves, chopped (7 Calories, Caloric Ratio: Carbohydrate 70%, Fat 23%, Protein 7%)
3 oz gruyère cheese, grated (270 Calories, Caloric Ratio: Carbohydrate 5%, Fat 69%, Protein 26%); alternatively: 3 oz comté cheese, grated (360 Calories, Caloric Ratio: Fat 72%, Protein 28%)
2 oz parmigiano reggiano cheese, grated (220 Calories, Caloric Ratio: Fat 67%, Protein 33%)
Optional: kosher salt and black pepper to taste

Directions

Preheat your Air Fryer to 400°F.

Make evenly-sliced potatoes ($\frac{1}{8}$th- to $\frac{1}{4}$th-inch thick) using a mandolin slicer.

In a bowl, combine two kinds of cheese then transfer $\frac{1}{3}$ of the mixture into a separate bowl and set aside for a while.

Pour cream into the first bowl then add garlic and thyme. Season generously with salt and pepper. Add potato slices and toss until every slice is coated with the cream/cheese mixture.

Grease the Fry Basket Grease then lay potato slices onto it, organizing them into a horizontally aligned neat stack. It's important to arrange sliced potatoes very tightly. Pour the cream/cheese mixture evenly over a potato layer then add another layer of potato slices and pour the mixture again. Repeat with the remaining potato slices. You do not need to use all excess mixture.

Place the Basket into your Air Fryer (do not preheat). Air fry for about 20 minutes, until pale golden brown. Remove the Basket, sprinkle casserole with the remaining mixture of two kinds of cheese, and return to your Air Fryer. Continue frying for another few minutes.

Remove the Basket, carefully place casserole in a serving dish. Serve warm.

29. Stuffed Sweet Potatoes

Preparation time: 10 minutes
Cooking time: 45 minutes
Servings: 4
Nutrition per serving: Calories **752**   Calories from Fat **316**

Ingredients
4 sweet potatoes, large (440 Calories, Caloric Ratio: Carbohydrate 94%, Protein 6%)
1 large onion, chopped (63 Calories, Caloric Ratio: Carbohydrate 92%, Fat 2%, Protein 6%)
1 chili pepper, chopped (18 Calories, Caloric Ratio: Carbohydrate 79%, Fat 9%, Protein 12%)
1 lbs minced beef (1310 Calories, Caloric Ratio: Fat 33%, Protein 67%)
1 tablespoons Cajun seasoning (0 Calories, Caloric Ratio: Carbohydrate 100%)
½ can (14 oz) crushed tomatoes (126 Calories, Caloric Ratio: Carbohydrate 81%, Fat 7%, Protein 12%)

1 cup kidney beans, canned (210 Calories, Caloric Ratio: Carbohydrate 72%, Fat 6%, Protein 22%)
½ cup sour cream (246 Calories, Caloric Ratio: Carbohydrate 8%, Fat 86%, Protein 6%)
5 tablespoons olive oil (595 Calories, Caloric Ratio: Fat 100%)

Directions

Preheat your Air Fryer to 350°F.

During this time, prick potatoes before they are cooking, Place them into the Fry Basket. Spray your Air Fryer with 1 tablespoon of olive oil using cooking spray then place the Basket or Rack into the Fryer.

Air fry for 45 minutes until tender and soft. Give them the shake three times through cooking thus distributing the heat more evenly.

In the meantime, pour 4 tablespoons of olive oil in a pan. Heat this over medium heat until hot then cook onion and chili pepper for about 4 minutes until soft. Add beef and Cajun seasoning, and cook for about 5 minutes, stirring constantly. Finally, add tomatoes and kidney beans, bring it up to a simmer then gently cook for 30 minutes.

Once the potatoes and meat mixture are done, remove the potatoes from the Basket onto a serving dish then slice them in half lengthwise and pierce the meat mixture with a knife and spoon.

Serve warm with sour cream on top.

30. Avocado Fries

Preparation time: 10 minutes
Cooking time: 10 minutes
Servings: 2
Nutrition per serving: Calories **376**   Calories from Fat **204**

Ingredients
½ cup breadcrumbs (140 Calories, Caloric Ratio: Carbohydrate 88%, Protein 12%)
½ teaspoon salt (0 Calories, Caloric Ratio: Carbohydrate 100%)
1 avocado, peeled and sliced (322 Calories, Caloric Ratio: Carbohydrate 19%, Fat 77%, Protein 4%)
½ lime, juiced (5 Calories, Caloric Ratio: Carbohydrate 91%, Fat 2%, Protein 7%)
¼ cup all purpose flour (100 Calories, Caloric Ratio: Carbohydrate 88%, Protein 12%)
1 egg, medium (65 Calories, Caloric Ratio: Carbohydrate 2%, Fat 63%, Protein 35%)
1 tablespoon olive oil (119 Calories, Caloric Ratio: Fat 100%)
Optional: salt and black pepper to taste

Directions
In a shallow bowl, toss together breadcrumbs, salt, and pepper.
Crack an egg then place in a deep plate.
Squeeze fresh lime juice on avocado slices. Dredge in flour then dip in egg, and coat thoroughly in breadcrumbs.

Transfer the slices onto the bottom of the Fry Basket and spread out into 1 layer then spray it with 1 tablespoon of oil and place the Basket into your Air Fryer.

Air fry for 10 minutes (do not preheat) at 390°F, until the avocado slices are golden and crispy. Turn them over once half way through cooking.

Serve warm with your favorite dipping sauce.

31. Reuben Casserole

Preparation time: 15 minutes
Cooking time: 20 minutes
Servings: 4
Nutrition per serving: Calories **1124**   Calories from Fat **646**

Ingredients
1½ lbs raw uncooked pork sausages (2068 Calories, Caloric Ratio: Fat 79%, Protein 21%)
15 oz sauerkraut (135 Calories, Caloric Ratio: Carbohydrate 82%, Protein 18%)
1⅓ cups whole milk (195 Calories, Caloric Ratio: Carbohydrate 30%, Fat 49%, Protein 21%)
2 cups Swiss cheese, shredded (820 Calories, Caloric Ratio: Carbohydrate 5%, Fat 64%, Protein 31%)
6 regular slices rye bread, cubed (402 Calories, Caloric Ratio: Carbohydrate 75%, Fat 12%, Protein 13%)
20 oz (2¼ cups) cream of mushroom soup, canned, condensed (480 Calories, Caloric Ratio: Carbohydrate 75%, Fat 12%, Protein 13%)
1 tablespoon Dijon mustard (12 Calories, Caloric Ratio: Carbohydrate 42%, Fat 37%, Protein 21%)
½ cups onion, finely chopped (34 Calories, Caloric Ratio: Carbohydrate 92%, Fat 2%, Protein 6%)
⅔ cup egg noodles (147 Calories, Caloric Ratio: Carbohydrate 73%, Fat 12%, Protein 15%)
2 tablespoons butter, melted (204 Calories, Caloric Ratio: Fat 99%, Protein 1%)

Directions

Preheat your Air Fryer to 400°F.
Place melted butter bread cubes onto the bottom of a casserole that fits into your Air Fryer. Spread sauerkraut evenly over them then cut sausages into 2-in rounds and layer them over sauerkraut. Sprinkle shredded cheese over the sauerkraut.
In a large bowl, pour milk and soup. Mix well then add mustard and onion. Mix to distribute evenly then cover with noodles. Place the noodle mixture onto the casserole dish.
Carefully set casserole into your Air Fryer Basket then place the Basket into the Fryer.
Air fry for about 20 minutes.
Serve hot.

32. Easy Steak with Mushrooms

Preparation time: 15 minutes
Cooking time: 10 minutes
Servings: 2
Nutrition per serving: Calories **324**   Calories from Fat **199**

Ingredients
½ lbs boneless beef steak (440 Calories, Caloric Ratio: Fat 62%, Protein 38%)
8 oz mushrooms, sliced (48 Calories, Caloric Ratio: Carbohydrate 52%, Fat 13%, Protein 35%)
½ large onion, chopped (32 Calories, Caloric Ratio: Carbohydrate 92%, Fat 2%, Protein 6%)
2 garlic cloves, minced (8 Calories, Caloric Ratio: Carbohydrate 85%, Fat 3%, Protein 12%)
1 tablespoon olive oil (119 Calories, Caloric Ratio: Fat 100%)
Optional: salt and pepper to taste

Directions
Preheat your Air Fryer to 350°F.
Remove fat from the beef and slice it. In a bowl, season the slices with salt and pepper then add minced garlic. Be sure to

toss well to coat every slice then set aside for a while (5 to 10 minutes).

Place the beef into the Fry Basket then pour olive oil and place the Basket into your Air Fryer.

Air fry for about 5 minutes. Turn the slices over once half way through cooking.

Remove the Basket, add in mushrooms and onion, stir well, and return to your Air Fryer. Continue frying for another 5 minutes.

Serve warm with your choice of bread, rice, or salad.

33. Chipotle Beef

Preparation time: 15 minutes
Cooking time: 30 minutes
Servings: 5
Nutrition per serving: Calories **419**   Calories from Fat **135**

Ingredients
3 lbs beef eye of round (1743 Calories, Caloric Ratio: Fat 24%, Protein 76%)
5 cloves garlic, chopped (20 Calories, Caloric Ratio: Carbohydrate 85%, Fat 3%, Protein 12%)
1 tablespoon ground cumin (6 Calories, Caloric Ratio: Carbohydrate 34%, Fat 50%, Protein 16%)
3 tablespoon chipotle peppers in adobo sauce (22 Calories, Caloric Ratio: Carbohydrate 49%, Fat 27%, Protein 24%)
½ teaspoon ground cloves (4 Calories, Caloric Ratio: Carbohydrate 45%, Fat 52%, Protein 3%)
½ teaspoon paprika (3 Calories, Caloric Ratio: Carbohydrate 45%, Fat 38%, Protein 17%)
2 tablespoons fresh lime juice (8 Calories, Caloric Ratio: Carbohydrate 91%, Fat 2%, Protein 7%)
1 tablespoon ground oregano (27 Calories, Caloric Ratio: Carbohydrate 63%, Fat 28%, Protein 9%)
½ medium onion, chopped (23 Calories, Caloric Ratio: Carbohydrate 92%, Fat 2%, Protein 6%)
3 bay leaves (0 Calories, Caloric Ratio: Carbohydrate 100%)
1 cup water (0 Calories, Caloric Ratio: Carbohydrate 100%)

2 ½ teaspoons kosher salt (0 Calories, Caloric Ratio: Carbohydrate 100%)
2 tablespoons olive oil (238 Calories, Caloric Ratio: Fat 100%)
Optional: black pepper to taste

Directions
Preheat your Air Fryer to 400°F.
In a food processor, pour water and lime juice then add garlic, cumin, oregano, paprika, onion, chipotles, and cloves. Blend for about 1 minute until smooth.
Remove fat from the beef and cube it into medium size pieces. In a bowl, season the beef with salt and pepper. Be sure to toss well to coat every piece.
Place the beef into the Fry Basket then pour olive oil and place the Basket into your Air Fryer.
Air fry for about 5 minutes. Mix the beef once half way through cooking.
Pour the chipotle mixture over beef in the pot then add bay leaves. Gently stir to dredge the meat.
Air fry for about 25 minutes until the meat is tender. Stir twice through cooking thus distributing the heat more evenly.
Discard bay leaves. Remove beef then cool slightly. Skim fat from cooking juices. Shred beef with two forks. Return beef and cooking juices to slow cooker; heat through. Serve with rice. If desired, top with cheese and sour cream.
Once it is done, remove from the Fryer then place on a serving tray and discard bay leaves. Serve with rice, top with cheese and sour cream, if desired.

34. Steak and Pepper Sauce with Fried Chips

Preparation time: 20 minutes
Cooking time: 30 minutes
Servings: 4
Nutrition per serving: Calories **464**   Calories from Fat **134**

Ingredients
4 (6 to 8 oz each) beef fillet steaks (720 Calories, Caloric Ratio: Fat 32%, Protein 68%)
1 tablespoon light thickened cream (29 Calories, Caloric Ratio: Carbohydrate 8%, Fat 87%, Protein 5%)
4 potatoes 'Desiree', large (657 Calories, Caloric Ratio: Carbohydrate 98%, Protein 2%)
½ can (1.76 oz) green peppercorns (140 Calories, Caloric Ratio: Carbohydrate 69%, Fat 11%, Protein 20%)
1 tablespoon white balsamic vinegar (20 Calories, Caloric Ratio: Carbohydrate 100%)
¼ cup chicken stock (3 Calories, Caloric Ratio: Carbohydrate 50%, Fat 22%, Protein 28%)
1 tablespoon reduced-fat milk (8 Calories, Caloric Ratio: Carbohydrate 37%, Fat 36%, Protein 27%)
2 sprigs fresh thyme (32 Calories, Caloric Ratio: Carbohydrate 13%, Fat 71%, Protein 16%)
¼ teaspoon gluten-free corn flour (7 Calories, Caloric Ratio: Carbohydrate 81%, Fat 8%, Protein 11%)

2 tablespoons extra virgin olive oil (238 Calories, Caloric Ratio: Fat 100%)
Optional: salt and pepper to taste
Steamed green beans, to serve

Directions

Preheat your Air Fryer to 400°F.
Peel the potatoes and cut into thin slices then drizzle with 1 tablespoon of oil.
Place the slices into the Fry Basket then sprinkle salt and pepper over the potatoes. Place the Basket into your Air Fryer. Air fry for about 5 minutes then remove from the Fryer and place on a kitchen tissue; set aside for a while.
In a mixing bowl, combine peppercorns, cream, vinegar, milk, thyme, flour, and chicken stock. Stir for several minutes until sauce thickens.
Add beef steaks into the mixture then mix to distribute evenly. Let meat sit out for 10 to 20 minutes to marinate and make steaks more tender and flavorful.
Place the steaks into the Fry Basket and air fry for about 10 minutes. Turn them over and air fry for 5 minutes more.
Serve hot steaks with potato chips and beans.

35. Glazed Salmon

Preparation time: 10 minutes
Cooking time: 24 minutes
Servings: 4
Nutrition per serving: Calories **139**   Calories from Fat **25**

Ingredients
4 salmon fillets (5 oz each) (396 Calories, Caloric Ratio: Fat 14%, Protein 86%)
1 tablespoon chopped oregano (18 Calories, Caloric Ratio: Carbohydrate 63%, Fat 28%, Protein 9%)
Glaze
1 clove garlic, minced (4 Calories, Caloric Ratio: Carbohydrate 85%, Fat 3%, Protein 12%)
1 tablespoon honey (64 Calories, Caloric Ratio: Carbohydrate 100%)
2 teaspoons mirin (15 Calories, Caloric Ratio: Carbohydrate 100%)
1 tablespoon white wine (12 Calories, Caloric Ratio: Carbohydrate 12%, Protein 88%)
2 teaspoons soy sauce (5 Calories, Caloric Ratio: Carbohydrate 54%, Fat 1%, Protein 45%)
½ teaspoon ginger root (fresh), minced (1 Calories, Caloric Ratio: Carbohydrate 85%, Fat 8%, Protein 7%)
1 teaspoon sesame oil (40 Calories, Caloric Ratio: Fat 100%)
salt and pepper to taste

Directions

Preheat your Air Fryer to 400°F.

In a small saucepan with a cooking spray, cook and stir garlic over medium heat until soft (for about 3 minutes). Pour white wine and soy sauce, add honey, ginger, mirin, and salt and pepper then simmer for about 3 minutes until slightly thickened.

Brush fillets with this glaze, and sprinkle with oregano. Let salmon sit out for 10 to 30 minutes then, using a spatula, transfer fillets into the Fry Basket, pour sesame oil and place the Basket into your Air Fryer.

Air fry for about 8 minutes.

Serve with rice and enjoy warm.

36. Miso Tilapia

Preparation time: 5 minutes
Cooking time: 12 minutes
Servings: 4
Nutrition per serving: Calories **278**   Calories from Fat **27**

Directions
4 tilapia fillets (4 oz each) (400 Calories, Caloric Ratio: Fat 22%, Protein 78%)
2 garlic cloves, minced (8 Calories, Caloric Ratio: Carbohydrate 85%, Fat 3%, Protein 12%)
½ cup scallion, chopped (16 Calories, Caloric Ratio: Carbohydrate 82%, Fat 5%, Protein 13%)
¼ cup white miso (180 Calories, Caloric Ratio: Carbohydrate 100%)
½ cup mirin (360 Calories, Caloric Ratio: Carbohydrate 100%)
2 teaspoons ginger root (fresh), finely grated (4 Calories, Caloric Ratio: Carbohydrate 85%, Fat 8%, Protein 7%)

2 limes, 1 juiced and 1 cut into wedges (20 Calories, Caloric Ratio: Carbohydrate 91%, Fat 2%, Protein 7%)
2 tablespoons packed brown sugar (102 Calories, Caloric Ratio: Carbohydrate 100%)
½ teaspoon sesame oil (20 Calories, Caloric Ratio: Fat 100%)

Directions
In a small bowl, combine miso, mirin, lime juice, ginger, garlic, and sugar. Rub the miso mixture into the tilapia chunks. Thereafter, preheat your Air Fryer to 375°F.
Transfer the tilapia onto the bottom of the Fry Basket then spray it lightly with oil and place the Basket into your Air Fryer. Air fry for 5 to 6 minutes, pull out the Basket Assembly, turn the chunks over, and Air fry for another 5 to 6 minutes.
Serve with scallions, lime wedges on top. Enjoy warm. Serve with rice, if desired.

Vegetarian Lunch/Dinner

37. Herby Veggie Falafel with Pumpkin Sauce

Preparation time: 15 minutes
Cooking time: 10 minutes
Servings: 4
Nutrition per serving: Calories **264**   Calories from Fat **125**

Ingredients
2 white potatoes, small, peeled, grated (238 Calories, Caloric Ratio: Carbohydrate 90%, Fat 1%, Protein 9%)
2 carrots, medium, grated (50 Calories, Caloric Ratio: Carbohydrate 90%, Fat 5%, Protein 5%)
2 tablespoons cilantro (coriander) (½ Calories, Caloric Ratio: Carbohydrate 57%, Fat 19%, Protein 24%)
1 egg, medium (65 Calories, Caloric Ratio: Carbohydrate 2%, Fat 63%, Protein 35%)
1 head cabbage, small, shredded (171 Calories, Caloric Ratio: Carbohydrate 83%, Fat 4%, Protein 13%)
½ small papaya, peeled, grated (30 Calories, Caloric Ratio: Carbohydrate 91%, Fat 3%, Protein 6%)
2 tablespoons almond flour (85 Calories, Caloric Ratio: Carbohydrate 12%, Fat 75%, Protein 13%)

½ teaspoon baking soda (0 Calories, Caloric Ratio: Carbohydrate 100%)
1 large onion, diced (63 Calories, Caloric Ratio: Carbohydrate 92%, Fat 2%, Protein 6%)
2 tablespoons vegetable oil (240 Calories, Caloric Ratio: Fat 100%)
Optional: salt to taste

Sauce
1 clove garlic, minced (4 Calories, Caloric Ratio: Carbohydrate 85%, Fat 3%, Protein 12%)
1 tablespoon butter (102 Calories, Caloric Ratio: Fat 99%, Protein 1%)
1 cup pumpkin purée (115 Calories, Caloric Ratio: Carbohydrate 62%, Fat 30%, Protein 8%)
1 cup chicken broth (10 Calories, Caloric Ratio: Carbohydrate 32%, Fat 36%, Protein 32%)
¼ teaspoon ground nutmeg (3 Calorie, Caloric Ratio: Carbohydrate 38%, Fat 58%, Protein 4%)
¼ teaspoon chili powder (2 Calorie, Caloric Ratio: Carbohydrate 42%, Fat 45%, Protein 13%)

Directions
Preheat your Air Fryer to 320°F.
Crack an egg then place in a bowl. Season with salt, coriander, baking soda then whisk until incorporated.
Add the shredded cabbage, grated papaya, carrots, potatoes, almond flour and onion to the bowl. Mix well and form into round or flat falafel.
Arrange the falafel in the Fry Basket. Spray your Air Fryer with oil using cooking spray then place the Basket into the Fryer. Air fry for about 5 minutes, until deep brown and crisp. Turn the falafel over once half way through cooking.
While waiting for the falafel, prepare the sauce. Place garlic onto a large skillet with butter. Sauté over medium heat for about 2 minutes, until the garlic is soft and fragrant. Add the pumpkin purée and chicken broth to the skillet then stir to combine. Add the nutmeg and chili powder. Simmer over medium heat, stirring occasionally, for about 10 minutes.
Serve warm falafel with the sauce.

38. Falafel with Tahini Sauce

Preparation time: 45 min
Cooking time: 15 min
Servings: 4
Nutrition per serving: Calories **177**   Calories from Fat **107**

Ingredients
Falafel
1 teaspoon ground cumin (2 Calories, Caloric Ratio: Carbohydrate 34%, Fat 50%, Protein 16%)
½ cup chickpeas, soaked overnight (110 Calories, Caloric Ratio: Carbohydrate 63%, Fat 16%, Protein 21%)
½ teaspoon coriander seeds (3 Calories, Caloric Ratio: Carbohydrate 36%, Fat 50%, Protein 14%)
½ teaspoon turmeric (4 Calories, Caloric Ratio: Carbohydrate 70%, Fat 23%, Protein 7%)
1 heaped tablespoon tahini (105 Calories, Caloric Ratio: Carbohydrate 6%, Fat 77%, Protein 17%)
½ teaspoon tamari soybean sauce (3 Calories, Caloric Ratio: Carbohydrate 100%)
½ teaspoon crushed red pepper flakes (2 Calories, Caloric Ratio: Carbohydrate 53%, Fat 36%, Protein 11%)
3 cloves garlic, chopped (12 Calories, Caloric Ratio: Carbohydrate 85%, Fat 3%, Protein 12%)

4 tablespoon parsley, finely chopped (4 Calorie, Caloric Ratio: Carbohydrate 63%, Fat 18%, Protein 19%)
½ large onion, diced (32 Calories, Caloric Ratio: Carbohydrate 92%, Fat 2%, Protein 6%)
½ lemon, juiced (10 Calorie, Caloric Ratio: Carbohydrate 84%, Fat 6%, Protein 10%)
2 tablespoons fava bean flour (55 Calories, Caloric Ratio: Carbohydrate 65%, Fat 4%, Protein 31%)
2 tablespoons olive oil (238 Calories, Caloric Ratio: Fat 100%)
Optional: salt to taste (approx. ½ tsp)

Tahini Sauce
1 clove garlic, minced (4 Calories, Caloric Ratio: Carbohydrate 85%, Fat 3%, Protein 12%)
½ lemon, juiced (10 Calorie, Caloric Ratio: Carbohydrate 84%, Fat 6%, Protein 10%)
1 heaped tablespoon tahini (105 Calories, Caloric Ratio: Carbohydrate 6%, Fat 77%, Protein 17%)
½ teaspoon hot chilli sauce (3 Calories, Caloric Ratio: Carbohydrate 33%, Protein 67%)
½ teaspoon tamari soybean sauce (3 Calories, Caloric Ratio: Carbohydrate 100%)
1 tablespoon parsley, finely chopped (1 Calorie, Caloric Ratio: Carbohydrate 63%, Fat 18%, Protein 19%)
pinch of salt (0 Calories, Caloric Ratio: Carbohydrate 100%)
1 tablespoon water (0 Calories, Caloric Ratio: Carbohydrate 100%)

Direction
Air fry cumin and coriander seeds at 320°F for a few minutes until fragrant then place them in a mortar and mash with a pestle.
Once the chickpeas beans have soaked, drain and rinse them well in a colander then transfer to a bowl.
Finely chop onion, place it onto the bottom of the Fry Basket and spread out into 1 layer then spray it lightly with 1 tablespoon of oil then place the Basket into your Air Fryer. Air fry at 350°F for a few minutes until softened.
Use a kitchen blender to grind chickpeas with lemon juice, tamari, garlic, tahini, and parsley until you get a smooth

texture then place in a mixing bowl and stir in the remaining ingredients.

Set aside in the fridge to firm up for about 30 minutes, then roll into ping pong size round or oval shaped Falafel balls.

Heat the oil in a pan (I use a high side sauce pan). You should use enough oil to totally immerse the falafels.

Arrange the falafel in the Fry Basket. Spray your Air Fryer with 1 tablespoon of oil using cooking spray then place the Basket into the Fryer.

Air fry at 350°F for about 10 minutes, until deep brown and crisp. Turn the falafel over once half way through cooking.

While waiting for the falafel, prepare the sauce. In a small bowl, combine tahini, lemon juice, tamari, and chilli sauce. Mix well until the mixture thickens. Stir in garlic and salt, add water to thin it a little and make a smooth sauce that's just the right consistency for drizzling then add parsley.

Serve warm falafel with the sauce.

39. Broccoli with Parmesan Cheese

Preparation time: 10 minutes
Cooking time: 8 minutes
Servings: 3
Nutrition per serving: Calories **212**   Calories from Fat **109**

Ingredients
1 broccoli bunch (approx. 1⅓ lbs) (207 Calorie, Caloric Ratio: Carbohydrate 70%, Fat 9%, Protein 21%)
¼ cup shaved parmesan cheese (or vegetarian alternative) (90 Calorie, Caloric Ratio: Carbohydrate 5%, Fat 57%, Protein 38%)
2 tablespoons olive oil (238 Calories, Caloric Ratio: Fat 100%)
½ cup marinara sauce (80 Calorie, Caloric Ratio: Carbohydrate 67%, Fat 23%, Protein 10%)
1 tablespoon lemon juice (12 Calories, Caloric Ratio: Carbohydrate 93%, Protein 7%)
2 cloves garlic, minced (8 Calories, Caloric Ratio: Carbohydrate 85%, Fat 3%, Protein 12%)
½ teaspoon ground black pepper (0 Calories, Caloric Ratio: Carbohydrate 100%)
½ teaspoon kosher salt (0 Calories, Caloric Ratio: Carbohydrate 100%)

Directions
Cut broccoli into bite size pieces then bring into a saucepan filled with water and boil over high heat for 2 minutes. Drain the broccoli and transfer it to a bowl then season with salt and

pepper. Mince garlic and toss it in with the broccoli. Drizzle 1 tablespoon oil over the broccoli.

Set the Air Fryer to 400°F and place the broccoli in the Fry Basket. Spray your Air Fryer with 1 tablespoon of oil using cooking spray then place the Basket into the Fryer.

Air fry for about 4 minutes, turning them over once half way through cooking.

Once the pieces are evenly brown, remove the Basket from the Air Fryer then add the shredded cheese and marinara sauce on top.

Place the broccoli back into the Air Fryer. Air fry just for a couple of minutes at 400°F.

Pour lemon juice over the broccoli and serve immediately.

40. Easy Vegetarian Lasagna

Preparation time: 20 minutes
Cooking time: 40 minutes
Servings: 4
Nutrition per serving: Calories **399**   Calories from Fat **193**

Ingredients
2 large fresh lasagna pasta sheets, cut into halves (210 Calories, Caloric Ratio: Carbohydrate 82%, Fat 4%, Protein 14%)
⅓ cup capsicum, chopped (26 Calories, Caloric Ratio: Carbohydrate 83%, Fat 10%, Protein 7%)
⅓ cup onion, chopped (15 Calories, Caloric Ratio: Carbohydrate 92%, Fat 2%, Protein 6%)
½ cup whole leaf spinach, shredded (20 Calories, Caloric Ratio: Carbohydrate 60%, Protein 40%)
½ can (14 oz) crushed tomatoes (126 Calories, Caloric Ratio: Carbohydrate 81%, Fat 7%, Protein 12%)
3 tablespoons tomato puree, canned or fresh (18 Calories, Caloric Ratio: Carbohydrate 81%, Fat 4%, Protein 15%)
½ cup shaved parmesan cheese (or vegetarian alternative) (180 Calorie, Caloric Ratio: Carbohydrate 5%, Fat 57%, Protein 38%)
½ cup part skim ricotta cheese (160 Calories, Caloric Ratio: Carbohydrate 30%, Fat 45%, Protein 25%)

2 zucchini, medium (62 Calories, Caloric Ratio: Carbohydrate 75%, Fat 9%, Protein 16%)
1 clove garlic, chopped (4 Calories, Caloric Ratio: Carbohydrate 85%, Fat 3%, Protein 12%)
2 tablespoons olive oil (238 Calories, Caloric Ratio: Fat 100%)
Optional: salt and black pepper to taste

<u>Béchamel sauce</u>
1½ cups buttermilk (Lowfat, Cultured) (147 Calories, Caloric Ratio: Carbohydrate 46%, Fat 19%, Protein 35%)
3 tablespoon white flour (84 Calories, Caloric Ratio: Carbohydrate 86%, Fat 2%, Protein 12%)
3 tablespoons unsalted butter (306 Calories, Caloric Ratio: Fat 99%, Protein 1%)

Directions
In a saucepan, warm milk and set aside for a while.
Heat butter gently over low heat in a separate saucepan until it has melted completely, but do not let it brown. Add flour and stir it quickly into the butter using a wooden spatula, until the mixture looks like wet scrambled eggs.
Heat the flour-butter roux over low heat for 5 to 8 minutes stirring constantly to make sure all bubbles get released (butter usually contains up to 20% of water, which starts to evaporate effectively once the butter reaches a temperature of 212°F). The mixture dries out and turns just a bit darker to a more "blond" or golden roux, where the flour has just been cooked.
Pour in a few tablespoons of the hot milk, just enough to moisten the flour-butter roux then stir thoroughly to loosen up the mixture then add the remaining milk and whisk vigorously until smooth.
Heat the roux over low heat, stirring constantly, until starting to bubble and thicken thus yielding a creamy mix of milk, flour, and butter. Add cheeses, salt, and pepper then set aside for a while.
To make tomato onion sauce, place chopped onion into a frying pan then pour olive oil. Sauté over medium-high heat until soft and golden brown. Add garlic then sauté for 1 minute. Add crushed tomatoes, 1 tablespoon of tomato puree,

and spinach then sauté until tender for approximately 5 minutes. Add salt and pepper then set aside for a while.
Peel zucchini then cut it into thin slices. Pour 2 tablespoon of tomato puree the slices and cubes aside for a while.
Preheat your Air Fryer to 375°F.
Take a baking tin or oven dish and grease it with oil. Spread the bottom with some tomato puree, top with first layer of lasagna sheet, spread zucchini and pour the remaining tomato puree over the layer, cover it with the second layer of lasagna sheet, spread a half of tomato onion sauce, top it with the third layer of lasagna sheet, spread the remaining tomato onion sauce then cover it with the fourth layer of lasagna sheet, spreading béchamel sauce with cheeses and capsicum on top.
Place the tin or dish in the Fry Basket then spray your Air Fryer with some oil and place the Basket into the Fryer.
Air fry for about 15 minutes.
Let rest 10 to 15 minutes before serving. Serve warm.

41. Zucchini and Halloumi Fritters

Preparation time: 10 minutes
Cooking time: 6 minutes
Servings: 4
Nutrition per serving: Calories **227**   Calories from Fat **130**

Ingredients
2 medium zucchini (unpeeled), grated (62 Calories, Caloric Ratio: Carbohydrate 75%, Fat 9%, Protein 16%)
1 medium carrot, grated (25 Calories, Caloric Ratio: Carbohydrate 90%, Fat 5%, Protein 5%)
5 oz halloumi cheese, grated (450 Calories, Caloric Ratio: Fat 75%, Protein 25%)
1 egg, medium (65 Calories, Caloric Ratio: Carbohydrate 2%, Fat 63%, Protein 35%)
¼ cup corn flour (110 Calories, Caloric Ratio: Carbohydrate 81%, Fat 8%, Protein 11%)
½ clove garlic, minced (2 Calories, Caloric Ratio: Carbohydrate 85%, Fat 3%, Protein 12%)
1 medium red onion, grated (46 Calories, Caloric Ratio: Carbohydrate 90%, Fat 2%, Protein 8%)
1 teaspoon ground oregano (9 Calories, Caloric Ratio: Carbohydrate 63%, Fat 28%, Protein 9%)
2 teaspoons coriander powder (5 Calories, Caloric Ratio: Carbohydrate 36%, Fat 50%, Protein 14%)

1 tablespoon lemon juice (12 Calories, Caloric Ratio: Carbohydrate 93%, Protein 7%)
1 teaspoon salt (0 Calories, Caloric Ratio: Carbohydrate 100%)
½ teaspoon black pepper (2½ Calories, Caloric Ratio: Carbohydrate 81%, Fat 11%, Protein 8%)
1 tablespoon olive oil (119 Calories, Caloric Ratio: Fat 100%)

Directions

In a bowl, place grated zucchini then sprinkle ½ teaspoon of salt and leave it to rest for about 15 minutes.

In 15 minutes, take a cheesecloth, remove zucchini from the bowl and place onto the cloth. Bundle it up then squeeze zucchini dry.

In the bowl, place carrot and onion then add the zucchini, flour, garlic, pepper, egg, oregano, coriander, and lemon juice. Add halloumi and season with ½ teaspoon of salt then mix well to combine into a consistent batter. Shape into round patties.

Preheat your Air Fryer to 400°F.

Arrange the fritters in the Fry Basket. Spray your Air Fryer with oil using cooking spray then place the Basket into the Fryer. Air fry for about 5 to 6 minutes, until golden brown. Turn the fritters over once half way through cooking.

Serve hot with yogurt.

42. Macaroni and Cheese Toasties

Preparation time: 5 minutes
Cooking time: 14 minutes
Servings: 1
Nutrition per serving: Calories **468**   Calories from Fat **204**

Ingredients
2 slices white bread (132 Calories, Caloric Ratio: Carbohydrate 78%, Fat 11%, Protein 11%)
1 egg, medium (65 Calories, Caloric Ratio: Carbohydrate 2%, Fat 63%, Protein 35%)
¼ cup macaroni pasta (55 Calories, Caloric Ratio: Carbohydrate 80%, Fat 5%, Protein 15%)
¼ cup ricotta cheese, grated (96 Calories, Caloric Ratio: Carbohydrate 11%, Fat 60%, Protein 29%)
3 tablespoons evaporated milk (60 Calories, Caloric Ratio: Carbohydrate 32%, Fat 47%, Protein 21%)
½ tablespoon olive oil (60 Calories, Caloric Ratio: Fat 100%)
Optional: salt and pepper to taste

Directions
Bring a pot of salted water to the boil then add pasta and cook for about 3 to 4 minutes; drain macaroni with strainer then set aside for a while.
In a mixing bowl, crack an egg and whisk until it gets light and fluffy then mix with evaporated milk.
Top the bread slice with ½ of the macaroni and cheese, just being similar to making a sandwich. Pour ½ of the egg mixture evenly over the top. Repeat layering two times. Place the other slice of bread on top and cut diagonally.
Preheat your Air Fryer to 350°F.
Place the toasties in the Fry Basket. Spray your Air Fryer with oil using cooking spray then place the Basket into the Fryer. Air fry for about 10 minutes, turning them over once half way through cooking.
Serve immediately.

43. Honey Cauliflower

Preparation time: 10 minutes
Cooking time: 20 minutes
Servings: 4
Nutrition per serving: Calories **300**   Calories from Fat **72**

Ingredients
1 head medium cauliflower, cut into florets (144 Calories, Caloric Ratio: Carbohydrate 76%, Fat 3%, Protein 21%)
⅓ cup gluten free oats (202 Calories, Caloric Ratio: Carbohydrate 70%, Fat 15%, Protein 15%)
½ cup plain flour (228 Calories, Caloric Ratio: Carbohydrate 86%, Fat 2%, Protein 12%)
¼ cup coconut, shredded (71 Calories, Caloric Ratio: Carbohydrate 18%, Fat 79%, Protein 3%)
½ teaspoon mustard (1½ Calories, Caloric Ratio: Carbohydrate 42%, Fat 37%, Protein 21%)
2 eggs, large (148 Calories, Caloric Ratio: Carbohydrate 2%, Fat 63%, Protein 35%)

¼ cup honey (256 Calories, Caloric Ratio: Carbohydrate 100%)
¼ cup evaporated milk (80 Calories, Caloric Ratio: Carbohydrate 32%, Fat 47%, Protein 21%)
½ tablespoon olive oil (60 Calories, Caloric Ratio: Fat 100%)
4 lettuce leaves (10 Calories, Caloric Ratio: Carbohydrate 67%, Protein 33%)
Optional: salt to taste

Directions
Preheat your Air Fryer to 350°F.
Crack eggs then place in a deep plate. In a mixing bowl, combine flour, oats, coconut, mustard, and salt. Dredge each piece of the cauliflower floret through the seasoned flour mixture, then jiggle it gently under the egg and flip, then put back into the flour mixture again.
Place the dressed florets in the Fry Basket. Spray your Air Fryer with oil using cooking spray then place the Basket into the Fryer.
Air fry for about 15 minutes.
While waiting for the cauliflower, prepare the honey sauce. Bring honey and milk to a boil in a medium saucepan over medium-high heat, stirring constantly then boil for about 2 minutes until sauce thickens. Set aside for a few minutes, allowing it to cool slightly.
Once it is done, remove the Fry Basket from the Air Fryer then set aside for a few minutes, allowing the cauliflower to cool down slightly before tossing in the sauce. When tossing, use tongs to stir until all of the cauliflower florets are completely coated with the honey sauce.
Place the dressed cauliflower back in the Air Fryer and air fry for 5 minutes at 350°F.
Serve warm on lettuce leaves.

44. Healthy Mediterranean Vegetables

Preparation time: 10 minutes
Cooking time: 15 minutes
Servings: 4
Nutrition per serving: Calories **134**   Calories from Fat **36**

Ingredients
2 oz cherry tomatoes, diced (10 Calories, Caloric Ratio: Carbohydrate 74%, Fat 9%, Protein 17%)
1 large courgette, sliced (52 Calories, Caloric Ratio: Carbohydrate 75%, Fat 9%, Protein 16%)
2 aubergines, sliced (132 Calories, Caloric Ratio: Carbohydrate 85%, Fat 7%, Protein 8%)
1 large green pepper, sliced (60 Calories, Caloric Ratio: Carbohydrate 83%, Fat 7%, Protein 10%)
1 medium carrot, diced (25 Calories, Caloric Ratio: Carbohydrate 90%, Fat 5%, Protein 5%)
2 oz parsnip, diced (42 Calories, Caloric Ratio: Carbohydrate 92%, Fat 3%, Protein 5%)
1 tablespoon honey (64 Calories, Caloric Ratio: Carbohydrate 100%)
1 teaspoon mustard (3 Calories, Caloric Ratio: Carbohydrate 42%, Fat 37%, Protein 21%)
2 tablespoons balsamic vinegar (26 Calories, Caloric Ratio: Carbohydrate 100%)
2 tablespoons fresh basil leaves, chopped (1 Calorie, Caloric Ratio: Carbohydrate 57%, Fat 19%, Protein 24%)

1 tablespoon olive oil (120 Calories, Caloric Ratio: Fat 100%)
Optional: salt to taste

Directions

Preheat your Air Fryer to 350°F.

Scatter courgettes, aubergines, green pepper, carrot, parsnip, and cherry tomatoes on the surface of the Fry Basket. Spray your Air Fryer with oil using cooking spray then place the Basket into the Fryer.

Air fry for about 15 minutes until the vegetables are just soft and tinged brown.

In the meantime, bring honey, mustard, and balsamic vinegar in a medium saucepan over low heat, stirring constantly and adding some water. Set aside for a few minutes, allowing it to cool.

Tip the vegetables into a serving dish, drizzle with the vinegar mixture, sprinkle basil on top then serve immediately.

45. Easy Crispy Tofu

Preparation time: 15 minutes
Cooking time: 20 minutes
Servings: 3
Nutrition per serving: Calories **408**   Calories from Fat **197**

Ingredients
1 block (14 oz) tofu (612 Calories, Caloric Ratio: Carbohydrate 13%, Fat 43%, Protein 44%)
2 tablespoons soy sauce (16 Calories, Caloric Ratio: Carbohydrate 54%, Fat 1%, Protein 45%)
1 teaspoon rice vinegar (0 Calories, Caloric Ratio: Carbohydrate 100%)
2 teaspoons toasted sesame oil (80 Calories, Caloric Ratio: Fat 100%)

1 tablespoon potato starch (40 Calories, Caloric Ratio: Carbohydrate 100%)
4 pouches (1 oz) agave syrup (80 Calories, Caloric Ratio: Carbohydrate 100%)
⅔ cup tomato paste (143 Calories, Caloric Ratio: Carbohydrate 82%, Fat 5%, Protein 13%)
½ lemon, juiced (10 Calorie, Caloric Ratio: Carbohydrate 84%, Fat 6%, Protein 10%)
1 teaspoon curry powder (6 Calorie, Caloric Ratio: Carbohydrate 52%, Fat 36%, Protein 12%)
2 tablespoons olive oil (238 Calories, Caloric Ratio: Fat 100%)
Optional: sea salt and freshly ground black pepper

Directions
Cube tofu and place in a bowl, add soy sauce, vinegar, sesame oil, salt, and pepper then very gently stir using a spatula. Set aside for 20 to 30 minutes.
Preheat your Air Fryer to 370°F.
Toss the marinated tofu with potato starch then transfer onto the bottom of the Fry Basket and place the Basket into the Fryer.
Air fry for about 20 minutes. Give the shake once half way through cooking.
In the meantime, make a flavorful curry ketchup. In a separate bowl, mix agave syrup, tomato paste, lemon juice, curry powder, and olive oil then add some water (2 to 3 tablespoons).
Serve warm tofu with the ketchup.

Quick and Easy Dessert Recipes

46. Banana Spring Rolls

Preparation time: 5 minutes
Cooking time: 7 minutes
Servings: 2
Nutrition per serving: Calories **462**   Calories from Fat **130**

Ingredients
2 large bananas (242 Calories, Caloric Ratio: Carbohydrate 92%, Fat 3%, Protein 5%)
8 spring roll wrappers (240 Calories, Caloric Ratio: Carbohydrate 93%, Protein 7%)
¼ cup brown sugar (135 Calories, Caloric Ratio: Carbohydrate 100%)
2 teaspoons toasted wheat germ (16 Calories, Caloric Ratio: Carbohydrate 49%, Fat 18%, Protein 33%)
¼ cup baking cocoa (40 Calories, Caloric Ratio: Carbohydrate 49%, Fat 27%, Protein 24%)
1 teaspoon vanilla extract (12 Calories, Caloric Ratio: Carbohydrate 17%, Protein 83%)
2 tablespoons peanut oil (238 Calories, Caloric Ratio: Fat 100%)

8 wooden skewers

Directions

Preheat your Air Fryer to 375°F.

Peel bananas, cut in half lengthwise then slice crosswise into quarters. Place them diagonally across the center of each wrapper then sprinkle with sugar, wheat germ, cocoa, and vanilla. Roll up spring roll wrappers from the corner to the center.

Now use the skewers to thread the rolls then place them into the Fry Basket. Spray your Air Fryer and the rolls with peanut oil using cooking spray then place the Basket into the Fryer. Air fry for about 5 to 7 minutes.

Serve warm or chilled.

47. Brown Sugar Peaches

Preparation time: 10 minutes
Cooking time: 30 minutes
Servings: 3
Nutrition per serving: Calories **233**   Calories from Fat **142**

Ingredients
3 fresh peaches, medium (114 Calories, Caloric Ratio: Carbohydrate 88%, Fat 5%, Protein 7%)
¼ cup brown sugar (135 Calories, Caloric Ratio: Carbohydrate 100%)
1 teaspoon ground cinnamon (5 Calories, Caloric Ratio: Carbohydrate 100%)
¼ cup pecans, chopped (206 Calories, Caloric Ratio: Carbohydrate 7%, Fat 88%, Protein 5%)
2 tablespoons peanut oil (238 Calories, Caloric Ratio: Fat 100%)

Directions
Preheat your Air Fryer to 320°F.
Cut peaches in half then place in the Baking Dish/Fry Basket, skin-side down. Sprinkle with sugar, cinnamon, and pecans. Spray your Air Fryer and the peaches with peanut oil using cooking spray then place the Dish/Basket into the Fryer.

Air fry for about 25 minutes until tender. To get browned crispy and crackling crust set temperature to 400°F then air fry for 5 more minutes.

Once it is done, let cool for about 10 minutes. Serve with an ice cream, if desired.

48. Chocolate Cake

Preparation time: 10 minutes
Cooking time: 20 minutes
Servings: 4
Nutrition per serving: Calories **428**   Calories from Fat **60**

Ingredients
1 cup plain flour (456 Calories, Caloric Ratio: Carbohydrate 86%, Fat 2%, Protein 12%)
1 cup granulated sugar (774 Calories, Caloric Ratio: Carbohydrate 100%)
2 eggs, large (148 Calories, Caloric Ratio: Carbohydrate 2%, Fat 63%, Protein 35%)
¼ cup baking cocoa (40 Calories, Caloric Ratio: Carbohydrate 49%, Fat 27%, Protein 24%)
½ teaspoon baking soda (0 Calories, Caloric Ratio: Carbohydrate 100%)
1 teaspoon baking powder (0 Calories, Caloric Ratio: Carbohydrate 100%)

1 tablespoon apricot jam (0 Calories, Caloric Ratio: Carbohydrate 100%)
pinch of salt (30 Calories, Caloric Ratio: Carbohydrate 100%)
½ cup buttermilk (Lowfat, Cultured) (49 Calories, Caloric Ratio: Carbohydrate 46%, Fat 19%, Protein 35%)
¼ cup powdered sugar (97 Calories, Caloric Ratio: Carbohydrate 100%)
1 tablespoon olive oil (119 Calories, Caloric Ratio: Fat 100%)

Directions
Preheat your Air Fryer to 320°F.
Crack eggs then place in a bowl. Season with salt then whisk until incorporated. Add flour, granulated sugar, cocoa, baking soda, and baking powder then pour milk, stir using a low-speed mixer, and knead a stiff, elastic dough. Add some water to a bowl and whisk until the right consistency of pancake batter. It should not be runny or watery, but very puffy-like. Take the Baking Dish and grease it with ½ tablespoon of olive oil using a cooking spray then pour the batter into it. Spray your Air Fryer with the remaining oil and place the Dish into the Fryer.
Bake the cake by air frying for about 15 to 20 minutes.
Remove the cake from the Air Fryer and turn it out of the Dish onto a cooling rack. Allow the cake to cool then sprinkle sugar powder on top. Serve with apricot jam.

49. Vegan Apple Turnover

Preparation time: about 30 minutes, excluding preparation and standing time for the dough
Cooking time: 15 minutes
Servings: 6
Nutrition per serving: Calories **446**   Calories from Fat **92**

Ingredients
Pastry dough
1 cup white wheat bread flour (495 Calories, Caloric Ratio: Carbohydrate 83%, Fat 4%, Protein 13%)
1 cup all-purpose flour (400 Calories, Caloric Ratio: Carbohydrate 88%, Protein 12%)
¼ cup vegan buttery sticks (400 Calories, Caloric Ratio: Fat 100%)
1 cup water (0 Calories, Caloric Ratio: Carbohydrate 100%)
1 teaspoon lemon juice (4 Calories, Caloric Ratio: Carbohydrate 93%, Protein 7%)
salt, to taste (½ to ⅔ teaspoons)
Alternatively, use frozen puff pastry sheets (approx. 10 oz)
Apple Filling
3 apples (Granny Smith or Honey Crisp), medium (210 Calories, Caloric Ratio: Carbohydrate 96%, Fat 3%, Protein 1%)
1 cup confectioners sugar (480 Calories, Caloric Ratio: Carbohydrate 100%)
1 cup brown sugar (540 Calories, Caloric Ratio: Carbohydrate 100%)

1 tablespoon lemon juice (12 Calories, Caloric Ratio: Carbohydrate 93%, Protein 7%)
1 teaspoon ground cinnamon (5 Calories, Caloric Ratio: Carbohydrate 100%)
½ teaspoon ground nutmeg (6 Calorie, Caloric Ratio: Carbohydrate 38%, Fat 58%, Protein 4%)
2 tablespoons almond milk (5 Calories, Caloric Ratio: Carbohydrate 12%, Fat 74%, Protein 14%)
¼ teaspoon salt (0 Calories, Caloric Ratio: Carbohydrate 100%)
2 cups water (0 Calories, Caloric Ratio: Carbohydrate 100%)
1 tablespoon olive oil (119 Calories, Caloric Ratio: Fat 100%)

Directions
Prepare the dough
In a mixing bowl, add the bread flour and all-purpose flour then season with salt and whisk to combine.
Place ⅓ of buttery sticks in the bowl and cut using a pastry cutter until the mixture has only tiny lumps of butter. Pour water and lemon juice then mix using the mixing spoon or stir using a low speed mixer until just combined. Quickly knead a stiff, elastic dough for about 30 seconds. The dough should not be watery, add up to ¼ cup of all-purpose flour in one tablespoon increments otherwise.
Lightly dust a work surface with flour and place a bowl of water nearby. Dip your hands in water then shake off the excess, and roll the dough into a ball. Tent loosely with cling foil then store in the fridge for about two hours.
Place the dough on a floured work surface then roll a lightly floured rolling pin out along approximately 12 to 12 inches square. Place some butter diagonally on top of the dough then fold the corners of the dough over the vegan butter, as if you're wrapping a gift then pinch the dough ends together to seal.
With a rolling pin, lightly tap the dough, from the center towards the edges, thus enlarging the square to about 14 inches then fold the dough in three folds like a tri-fold business letter. Fold the dough three times again, so it turns into a square. This counts as another turn. Tent loosely with cling foil

then store in the fridge for 1 more hour. This maintains the dough's strength making it more pliable.

Repeat the above dough turns two more times so you have reduced thickness of the dough and fat layers in the initial folded sandwich.

The resulting puff pastry can be stored in the fridge for up to 2 months. Just remove it from the fridge the night before cooking.

Prepare the filling

Preheat your Air Fryer to 400°F.

Wash, peel, core, and thinly slice apples then place slices into a medium mixing bowl. Pour water then add lemon juice and salt. Toss until well combined then set aside for about 15 minutes. Drain and set aside for a while.

In another bowl, combine the confectioners and brown sugar. Pour milk and stir until completely dissolved then add cinnamon and nutmeg; mix well.

Toss the apples in the sugar mixture until coated then put them all in the Baking Dish.

Place the Dish into your Air Fryer then air fry for about 5 minutes. Stir once half way through cooking.

Remove the Dish with the apple filling turn into mush from the Air Fryer and set aside on a cooling rack to cool.

Fill and fold the turnovers

Remove one of the puff pastry sheets from the refrigerator then cut into 4 inch squares. Put two tablespoons of the apple filling in the middle of each square. Fold one corner of the pastry over the filling, diagonally across to the opposite pastry edge, to form a triangle. Press down on the edges of the joined dough to seal. Repeat with the other dough squares and pastry sheets, until you reach desired number of turnovers.

Transfer them into the Fry Basket, spray your Air Fryer with oil, and place the Basket into the Fryer.

Set the temperature to 375°F then air fry for about 10 minutes. Serve warm or cold, as desired.

50. Vegan Anzac Cookies

Preparation time: 10 minutes
Cooking time: 10 minutes per one Baking Dish
Servings: 5
Nutrition per serving: Calories **476**   Calories from Fat **186**

Ingredients
1 cup quinoa flakes (390 Calories, Caloric Ratio: Carbohydrate 74%, Fat 14%, Protein 12%)
1 cup quinoa flour (440 Calories, Caloric Ratio: Carbohydrate 71%, Fat 13%, Protein 16%)
½ teaspoon baking soda (0 Calories, Caloric Ratio: Carbohydrate 100%)
2 tablespoons golden syrup (Lyle's) or honey (130 Calories, Caloric Ratio: Carbohydrate 100%)
¾ cup pure cane sugar or light brown sugar (540 Calories, Caloric Ratio: Carbohydrate 100%)
¼ cup unsweetened flaked coconut (100 Calories, Caloric Ratio: Carbohydrate 14%, Fat 82%, Protein 4%)
¼ cup roasted almonds (180 Calories, Caloric Ratio: Carbohydrate 10%, Fat 77%, Protein 13%)
¼ cup organic virgin coconut oil, warmed (480 Calories, Caloric Ratio: Fat 100%)
3 tablespoons water (0 Calories, Caloric Ratio: Carbohydrate 100%)
salt, to taste (¼ to ½ teaspoons)
1 tablespoon olive oil (119 Calories, Caloric Ratio: Fat 100%)

Optional: add up to ¼ cup golden raisins (Sun-Maid, 130 Calories, 0% Fat) and chopped macadamia nuts (Diamond of California, 220 Calories, 90% Fat), if desired

Directions

Preheat your Air Fryer to 350°F.

In a bowl, add quinoa flakes, quinoa flour, sugar, coconut, almonds, baking soda, and salt then mix until incorporated. Pour coconut oil, water, and syrup then whisk until well blended and of uniform consistency.

Add baking paper onto your Baking Dish/Fry Basket. Place the cookie dough onto the baking paper by 2-tablespoon scoops (alternatively, use an ice cream scooper), making sure they don't touch each other (with approx. 2-inch o.c. spacing). Spray your Air Fryer with olive oil and place the Dish into the Fryer.

Then air fry for about 8 to 10 minutes until the cookies are just starting to brown on the edges.

Remove the Dish from the Air Fryer and allow cookies to cool in the Dish for 5 minutes before removing to a rack to cool completely then serve.

Repeat cooking with the remaining cookie dough.

Conclusions

Once again, thank you for downloading this book!

We do hope this book inspires to make a successful plan for your daily meals using your Air fryer. Try these delicious recipes and enjoy the natural, fresh, and healthy foods filling your kitchen and making home cooking a pleasure every day!

Your Free Gift

We want to thank you for purchasing the book and would like to reward you with a valuable free gift

Food Styling Tips and Tricks

Just visit http://nb3publish.weebly.com to download it now.

We hope you enjoy it!

Thanks!

Archie Owens

Copyright 2017 by Archie Owens All rights reserved.
All rights Reserved. No part of this publication or the information in it may be quoted from or reproduced in any form by means such as printing, scanning, photocopying or otherwise without prior written permission of the copyright holder.

Disclaimer and Terms of Use: Effort has been made to ensure that the information in this book is accurate and complete, however, the author and the publisher do not warrant the accuracy of the information, text and graphics contained within the book due to the rapidly changing nature of science, research, known and unknown facts and internet. The Author and the publisher do not hold any responsibility for errors, omissions or contrary interpretation of the subject matter herein. This book is presented solely for motivational and informational purposes only.

Printed in Poland
by Amazon Fulfillment
Poland Sp. z o.o., Wrocław